SUCCEED
AS A
STRING
PLAYER!

TEEN STRINGS SHOWS YOU HOW....

EDITED BY Megan Westberg

STRING LETTER PUBLISHING

Publisher: David A. Lusterman
Editorial Director: Greg Cahill
Editor: Megan Westberg
Director of Production and Book Publishing: Ellen Richman
Designers: Barbara Summer and Timothy Jang
Photo Editor: Ray Larsen

Cover Image: Fiddler John Showman of the Creaking Tree String Quartet
Cover Photographer: Peter Moynes
Cover Design and Illustrations: Barbara Summer
Photo Credits: Bryant Rozier, p. 20; Leonard Yakir, p. 26; Michael Amsler, p. 76.

Library of Congress Cataloging-in-Publication Data
    Succeed as a String Player : Teen Strings Shows You How– / edited by
    Megan Westberg.
        p. cm.
    ISBN 978-1-890490-60-7 (pbk.)
    1. Bowed stringed instruments–Juvenile literature. 2. Bowed stringed
    instruments–Instruction and study–Juvenile. I. Westberg, Megan, 1980-
    II. Teen strings.
    MT259.S83 2007
    787'.193–dc22
                                2007033968

CONTENTS

Introduction

By Mimi Rabson

String playing is fun. It's really fun—making music, hearing the results of your efforts, stepping into the spotlight during a concert, creating something with your friends. It's fun to discover other cultures and ways of thinking through a common vocabulary, to be part of an art form that spans the entire globe and can be found throughout all human history.

It's hard, too. It's hard to get beautiful tone and perfect intonation and play those 16th-note runs just right. Like any acquired skill, it takes practice—that time-consuming process of combining intellect with muscle memory to make artistic expression effortless. Sometimes you make incremental steps. Sometimes there are long dry spells followed by giant leaps, but practicing does pay off. Each time you learn a new lick, a whole new realm of sounds, ideas, and opportunities opens up.

The possibilities are numerous and richly divergent for string players. You can be part of a non-competitive, creative body like an orchestra or chamber group, where each part is crucial to the success of the performance. You can play folk-dance music, where your skills must include propelling the dancing; make decisions in each measure about pitches, rhythms, and phrasing as you improvise; or pull out your electric instrument and rip it up with distortion and wah-wah pedals. You can be the center of attention as a soloist, drive the accompaniment, or round out the rhythm section.

There are so many ways to participate. Play with other people. Join an existing group. Start your own band. Sign up for the concert or the talent show. Listen to what you like the best and play it. Find a teacher who will help you grow. Prepare that audition. Take it to camp in the summer. Think about the music you are playing and figure out how it is put together. Make your own. Listen. Practice. Participate. Create.

Teen Strings magazine is the leader in providing access to information that concerns teen string players. Whether you're shopping for an electric instrument, preparing for an audition, or looking for some help with shifting, *Teen Strings* has the answers. This anthology puts current wisdom about playing a stringed instrument into one place. Browse through it or use it for specific research as you seek success in string playing. It'll be a valuable companion in your musical life.

Mimi Rabson is a violinist, violist, composer, and educator in the Boston area. She teaches at Berklee College of Music and regularly performs classical, jazz, klezmer, and other styles of music.

ROCK THE PRACTICE ROOM

DON'T GIVE UP!!!

You may think you can't do it,
but you can. There's a musician—
a string musician—burning,
yearning to play to its utmost
potential inside your heart
and soul.

— Chrissy, 15, violin

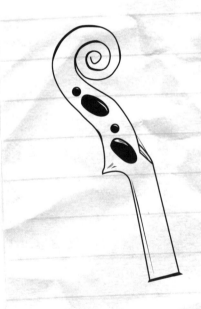

CHAPTER 1

GETTING IN TUNE

3 easy steps to better intonation
and a more productive practice regimen

By Rebecca Cole

Excellent intonation, consistently focused and accurate, is one of the foundations of good string playing. Unfortunately, poor intonation continues to plague many musicians despite hours of slow practicing, daily scales and arpeggios, and endless repetitions of problem notes. In addition to wasting time, many string players inadvertently reinforce problems because of the way they practice.

A common practice method involves repeating problematic notes or measures many times, expecting that each repetition will improve the intonation. The problem with this method is that these inaccurate repetitions form pathways in the brain that record the inaccurate intonation. As a result, during a performance, it is possible (if not probable) that your brain will instruct you to play out of tune.

Choosing to stop during practice to play a problem note several times usually fixes the problem only temporarily. Practicing slowly is a valuable technique, but is time-consuming and might not completely fix the problem. How can you practice intonation so the problems remain fixed?

1. Hear Thyself

Intonation work is most effective when it is part of a daily regimen. This regimen is individual, but needs to contain three elements: objective self-criticism to identify the problems, determination of the reasons for the problems (by asking specific questions), and practice that's designed to permanently fix problems. Unlike scales, arpeggios, and slow practicing, which work on several aspects of playing, an intonation regimen focuses only on intonation. According to neuroscientists studying motor skills, if you work on several skills simultaneously, you do not retain what you learn as well as if you focus on one skill at a time. So, focusing solely on intonation during part of your daily practice is the best way to improve it.

For your work, a good quality recording device (tape recorder or CD-RW) is important. Listening to a recording of your playing is the best way to objectively hear yourself and identify mistakes. In addition to investing in a recording device, take the time to make multiple copies of the music you're working on. Using these working copies keeps your original music from becoming cluttered with pencil marks, which can be distracting during a performance. These copies also create a record of your intonation work, so you can see patterns of mistakes, identify continuing problems, and chart your progress.

Begin your intonation work by recording one passage of music, no more than 32 measures long. Put down your instrument (to rest your hands and arms) and listen to your recording. As you listen, mark each intonation problem on a clean working copy. Using arrows above the note—up for sharp, down for flat, "U" for unclear—is an easy way to mark the music. (Write the date on this copy to help keep a record of when you practiced this passage.)

If you do not have a recording device, listen to your playing as if you were hearing someone else play across the room. While this is an excellent way to listen as you practice, it is very difficult to remember where each mistake occurred and  how the note was out of tune. For this step in your intonation work, you want to be as self-critical and objective as possible, so you can identify all mistakes.

2. Break It Down

The next step is analysis. For each mistake, create an excerpt beginning at least four notes before the out-of-tune note. Play your excerpt once or twice (no more) and ask yourself the following questions:

Where is the problem created? Is the problem the out-of-tune note only, or does a shift or string crossing preceding the note create the problem? A mistake is often the result of an earlier technical problem. Noticing what feels awkward, when you feel tense, or when you hold your breath will help you decide where the problem occurs.

What is the intonation problem? Is the note sharp, flat, or unfocused? Of course, your working copy shows these answers.

Is there a pattern? You might notice that a shift to third position precedes intonation mistakes. Once you recognize this pattern, you can work on learning the correct shift distance, then practice those shifts within your music. This is a very efficient way to practice. In addition, knowing a pattern helps you avoid repeating a similar mistake.

Recognizing that a shift is causing your problem is a good beginning. Not feeling the distance of the shift, not being able to shift fast enough, or not hearing the landing note within the harmony, is more specific information. This information will help you know how to practice to fix the problem.

Here are some techniques you can use to fix the problem: If you are having trouble judging the distance of a shift, so you land too flat or go too sharp, you need to teach your body to feel the shift distance. Practice the shift up and down using different rhythms. Also, practice going above or below where you want, then play the correct shift distance. It can also be helpful to play an arpeggio that contains that shift, or to play all the half-steps within the shift. Rather than repetition, try to find new ways to practice the same problem. If the problem is not fixed after a few repetitions, you need to find a different way to practice. You do not want to reinforce the mistake or develop a repetitive-stress or repetitive-motion injury.

> ## DID YOU KNOW?
> Italian violinist NICOLÒ PAGANINI (1782–1840) played with such force and velocity fans believed he was possessed by the devil. But those impressive skills had a much more earthly origin: Paganini was known to practice up to 15 hours a day to sharpen his fiddle attack.

3. Get Feedback

Once you feel comfortable with the excerpt, work on the next intonation problem. After you've finished practicing each intonation excerpt, play through the entire passage. Finish your work by playing the passage slowly to help reinforce what you learned.

An electronic tuner is sometimes used during intonation work. Here's an effective technique: close your eyes and play (at tempo) up to the note in question, then hold the note. Decide if it is sharp or flat, then look at the tuner to verify what you hear. This will gauge your ability to hear intonation. Of course, you still need to decide why the note was out of tune.

Finally, make a conscious habit of practicing easily, without tension or loud intense playing, during all of your intonation work. Consciously playing without force or tension may prevent repetitive-motion injuries. Loud practicing, especially for violin and viola players whose instrument is close to their ears, contributes to hearing loss.

The self-criticism, analysis of technical problems, and specific and varied practicing in this intonation regimen will improve your ability to hear intonation and to fix technical problems.

The focus, objective listening, and thoughtfulness you develop may extend to all of your practicing, improving other areas of your playing.

> **WISE WORDS**
>
> Playing the violin forces me to assess my own capacity to be truthful to myself and my abilities as a musician . . . it is impossible to improve and be dishonest.
>
> —*Leigh Mahoney, violinist and chamber musician*

CHAPTER 2

CREATIVE WOODSHEDDING

*Avoid drudgery to make better use
of your practice time*

By James Reel

Why do people give up playing after just a little study? Usually not because it's hard. Not because they hurt themselves. Not because instrument rental and lessons are too expensive.

No, the problem for most people is practicing. They want to play great, beautiful music, but what gets in the way is the daily drudgery of practicing. It's like having a chance to go back in time to help Antonio Stradivari create an instrument, but spending most of your visit watching the varnish dry.

It shouldn't be that way, says Philip Baldwin, assistant professor of violin and viola at Eastern Washington University. "Good practicing is creative practicing," he insists.

Practicing shouldn't be dull. But how do you make it more creative? Baldwin offers plenty of tips on how to avoid mindless repetition.

❝Good practicing is
creative practicing.❞
—Philip Baldwin

Make Your Mark

Mark bowings and fingerings in the score as soon as you decide on them; mark reference bowings so you can start in the middle of a phrase; use colored pencils for specific kinds of markings; use brackets to identify practice spots; mark tempos. Keep pencils handy, and use them! Then you can avoid wasting time figuring out the same things again and again.

Clear the Way

When it comes to learning notes efficiently, Baldwin advocates what he calls the "Zamboni Effect."

Zamboni is the make of the machine that cleans the ice at a skating rink.

"It eliminates all the grooves," Baldwin explains. "In music, the grooves are the mistakes or the miscoordinations that we make when we play. By completely reorganizing the way the music is practiced, your brain can learn in new ways; it's not stuck in its old ruts."

To achieve the Zamboni Effect, take a passage, eliminate the printed rhythm, and play the notes one at a time. Then regroup the notes into odd divisions, and practice this for awhile.

Train Your Ear

Take a high passage down an octave. Sing through a passage for pitch and musical contour. Close your eyes and just listen to a passage in your head. Sing and play at the same time.

SIMPLE IS BEST

The most useful thing I ever learned about solving technical problems is also the simplest: if you break it down, the problem is almost always between one note and one other note. The trick is to figure out which two notes are causing the trouble.

Isolate the problem spot and start there. Practice just the two notes, from one to the next, until you can nail it constantly. Of course, though it's simple, it's not always easy, but by isolating the problem we have a chance of solving it. When that's working, back up one note—just one—or expand out in both directions by one note, then two, then three, a measure on either side of the problem, until you can play the whole phrase without difficulty.

Find the next trouble spot and address it in the same way.

It might seem obvious, but how many times have we practiced a troublesome passage over and over without addressing the core problem, hoping the difficulty would disappear if only we practiced enough?

—*Erin Shrader*

The Big Picture

At all times, keep your mind in motion, right from the beginning of your practice session. Baldwin is especially fond of a line from Robert Gerle's *The Art of Practising the Violin*: "Think what you need to accomplish specifically during the day's practice: three minutes spent thinking about your practicing before you start are worth three hours spent in aimless repetition, during which you only learn the bad better."

CHAPTER 3

GOT TONE?

*Sound advice from the experts
on improving your tone production*

By Sarah Freiberg

"I find tone is like someone's voice," says virtuoso violinist Jaime Laredo, conductor of the prestigious New York String Orchestra Seminar, "and like appearances, no two sounds are alike." In other words, your tone is your musical voice, as individual as you are, and you want it to speak for you as clearly and articulately as possible.

The tools of sound production are few, the experts say, but their effects are endless. Sound depends on bow usage, and to a lesser extent, on vibrato. "To make a good sound, there are three basics: speed, pressure, and sounding point," says Muir Quartet violinist and Boston University professor Peter Zazofsky.

"The variety of each will present you with your best sound. What percentage of each depends on the context, but to find the right balance you have to manipulate each of these three variables."

To shape your tone, Laredo adds, you need to think about vibrato, the kind and amount of bow pressure you use, and most importantly, the bow speed. "I find that students often are concentrating on getting a big sound," he says, "but they should look instead to their bow speed. They often forget that they can get many varieties of sound by varying their bow speed."

A good tone, says violin teacher Emlyn Ngai of the Hartt School of Music, should have resonance. "If we approach the instrument and bow in the appropriate manner, we set the whole instrument vibrating," he explains.

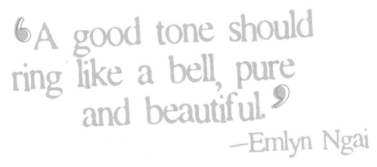

❝A good tone should ring like a bell, pure and beautiful.❞

—Emlyn Ngai

"A good tone should have a core in it for projection and warmth to please the listener's ear. A good tone should ring like a bell, pure and beautiful, even without the use of vibrato."

So how do you go about improving your sound?

Concert violinist and educator Ida Kavafian suggests that "warming up on long tones is a really good idea. We concentrate so much on the left hand, we forget to warm up the right. Work on smooth bow changes, loosening your fingers so that they can be responsive."

To understand tone production, Ngai adds, players should learn a bit about the physics and the physiology involved in playing a stringed instrument.

Once you grasp the physical aspects of playing, it's time to think about putting your warm-up sessions to better use. Dan Stepner, first violinist of the Lydian Quartet and concert-master of the Handel and Haydn Society, points out that daily practice and warm-up sessions offer opportunities to learn new pieces and to explore the tonal qualities of sound.

WISE WORDS

Sheer time is not necessarily good; what's good is the quality of the practicing. If somebody's really serious, five hours a day is almost too much; no more than that. After five hours, the body doesn't absorb anymore. When I was growing up, I didn't practice more than three hours a day. And when you practice, it's got to be 50-minute hours, with 10 minutes of rest.

—*Itzhak Perlman,*
violinist, on practice

In your search for your own great sound, it might be helpful to keep this thought from Kavafian in mind: "In terms of sound, your imagination is the most important component. Keep an open mind and explore every possibility.

"A person's imagination is his or her biggest asset."

BE a STaR

My most memorable playing experience
was the first time I played at a
nursing home during Christmastime.
I had performed many bigger concerts
and recitals that perhaps others would
say were more important. Playing there
made me feel good because I was doing
something nice for others, and it
was the first time that I felt like
I was truly using my art form for
someone who would really appreciate it.

— Heather, 15, violin

CHAPTER 4

STAYING COOL IN THE HOT SEAT

5 ways to get the most out of a master class

By Donna Shryer

On the surface, a master class seems to be about achieving perfection. Master teachers, however, say it's more about discovering possibilities. Let's examine both viewpoints. From a student's perspective (before reading this article, of course), a master class usually involves three to five students, and sometimes an audience, joining a respected master teacher who addresses one student at a time while the others listen. A student performs a prepared piece and the master advises. The student plays again, integrating the master's comments. Then there's more constructive criticism and more playing. So it goes, until desired results are achieved, and the master moves on to the next student.

It's easy to see how you might misinterpret the goal to be perfection.

Now let's look at the class from a master teacher's perspective. "Every piece has possibilities," says Kim Cook, professor of cello at Penn State University. "A master class gives you [the student]

an opportunity to try things from a fresh approach, get new ideas, and the teacher is there to help you see these possibilities. Sometimes you'll even hear things you already knew, but because they're explained in a new way, that light goes on.

"Connection!"

Making a focused connection with the music, Cook stresses, is what a master class is all about. Students shouldn't see constructive criticism as "do it again because you were bad," but rather "try it again because it could be better."

So, if you're getting ready to take a master class, an open mind to possibilities is the best way to maximize class time.

Here are five more ways to get the most from a master class.

1. Practice, Practice, Practice

"You've got to be really comfortable with the material," says Mimi Rabson, assistant violin professor at Berklee College of Music and a master-class teacher. "If the master says, 'Try it from here doing this,' and you're not well prepared, starting in the middle won't be an easy thing to do."

Rabson adds that improvising during practice is another way to up your preparedness. "Try a phrase with an up-bow instead of a down-bow. This is something a master teacher might suddenly suggest, and if you have the music inside you, this won't be a problem. If you're still struggling on a basic level, you won't be able to try things off the cuff."

2. Make Sure You Have Fresh Batteries

In other words, you should tape record the master class. You certainly can't take notes with an instrument in your hands. What's more, even the most relaxed master-class student won't be able to absorb all the information in one sitting. You can look forward to a few ah-ha moments when you connect so deeply to the master's advice that whatever's said next may be missed—because you're still back on the last point thinking, "Hey! This is cool."

> **"A master class gives you an opportunity to try things from a fresh approach."**
> —Kim Cook

3. Leave Your Nerves in the Instrument Case

To do this, think of a master class as a lesson that happens to be on a stage in front of people. This attitude may take some effort, since a master class does feel like a performance.

Here's how Rabson suggests you adjust your mind-set. "When you get out on a stage, you have to feel like king or queen of the universe. Inside your head you think 'I've got something to say and it's something really great.' When you get up front in a master class, it's more like, 'I've got something to say, but I think it could be better. Can you help me?'

"If you've made up your mind to think this way, nerves settle down."

4. Be Prepared for Nit-picking

In addition to viewing a master class as a lesson, you need to think of it as a lesson under a microscope. For example, when you play for an audience, everyone claps at the end of the recital and no one talks to you afterward about an F that was slightly out of tune. In a master class, it's all about that out-of-tune F. That's the point, and honest scrutiny is what you want.

A great way to prepare for the honest scrutiny is to sit in on a master-class audience before your big day, Cook recommends. "By observing a master class and getting familiar with the format, you'll see that everyone makes mistakes, and it's the master teacher's job to point them out. When it's your turn in the hot seat, you'll know that no one's picking on you. The teacher's doing his or her job!"

5. Turn to the Left and Say Hello

Even if you know your fellow master-class students by name, look forward to meeting them on a whole new level. This is everyone's chance to play their favorite piece, and it won't necessarily be what

TALK TO TEACHER

To find a master class, begin by talking to your teacher. If he or she does not host master classes, ask if he or she has a colleague who does. If you're involved in an orchestra situation, ask the orchestra teacher for a master-class connection. You might also contact the music school at a nearby conservatory, college, or university. At the teen level, there is generally no fee to attend a master class and auditions are not the norm—it's more about showing interest and then being invited to join.

—*D.S.*

you expect, making this a great opportunity to get up close with fellow students.

In addition, Rabson adds, it's a fabulous way to get ideas. "Maybe your background is classical music and suddenly you see students at your same level exploring other stuff. Hopefully you'll think, 'Hey, I can do that.' In a master-class setting, things don't seem so remote."

In one of Rabson's recent master classes, for example, someone played a movement from a Tchaikovsky concerto, the next student played a hip-hop piece for violin, someone else played a jazz standard, and someone else played an Astor Piazzolla tango. "It's so much fun for the students to see what their colleagues are doing," Rabson says. "And it all goes right back to the possibility of possibilities!"

CHAPTER 5

ALWAYS A WINNER

*Competing can be the best way to set goals
and hone your skills*

By Sarah-Hadley Yakir

I had never competed before even though I have practiced the violin seriously from the time I was four at the Special Music School in New York, and I had performed at lots of venues. I had traveled to Europe to study and attended summer music festivals since age eight. Competitions just were not something I was drawn to or felt ready for. But the Music Teachers National Association series, held in March at its National Student Competitions in Austin, Texas, was a great place to start.

A similar event at a teacher convention near home might be right for you, too. They feel very relaxed, but professional. For this competition, I competed by state first, then divisions of the country (like Eastern, Western, Southern, etc.), then nationals. Only the first-place winners proceed from one round to the next. The state and regional rounds of the Junior Division (ages 11–14) are held before the convention gets started, so things seem quiet and calm. You can stay focused and more relaxed. Every player is anonymous. The feedback from the adjudicators was spot-on and, in my case, instructive and encouraging.

I didn't listen to other players; I just concentrated on my music and on keeping my technique sharp. It paid off and I took first place in the 2006 MTNA Eastern Division. I had to give a winner's recital the same day, which was such fun with the charge of winning behind me.

The local paper ran an article and the mayor invited me to city hall, where I was presented with a certificate of achievement.

Sarah-Hadley Yakir

was then invited to perform in several concerts.

Students have to play the same program throughout all stages of the MTNA competitions. I worked the same program off and on for six months.

My teacher had me work on different concertos right after the rounds of the competition and then we came back to the original program a few weeks before each of the three rounds.

It was great to have a goal and to master the pieces in this way. All my practice hours became so focused: get this bow stroke, figure out the dynamics of that phrase, release tension, clean up that old problem that gets in the way of speed.

I could go on and on.

Through the process of competing, I learned how to slow down in the heat of the moment and really listen.

The last round presented some strange problems for me. I was starting to have a real growth spurt and I needed to move to a heavier, full-size bow and perhaps a full-size violin. Finding a bow that gave me the sound of my beloved 3/4-size bow that I could control was really tough; I almost shed a few tears traveling around to try new bows. My left hand started to lose its shape a little with so much focus on my bow arm.

As I grew, my intonation began to suffer, but I just knew I could not deal with too much change a few weeks before the national rounds.

We settled for a bow that was a little too inflexible for my Bach Partita, but was great for my Kreisler and Bruch, so I struggled to play lighter.

Despite the obstacles, I felt excited and ready to play the day of the finals. I did some yoga that morning and realized that the bow problem actually helped me to focus and work even harder to get the sound I wanted. Through the process of competing, I learned how to slow down in the heat of the moment and really listen. I learned to breathe and relax my arms in those moments when I could.

I learned to own the space I was in and felt proud to share my skills with those wanting to listen.

In the end, three very accomplished older players won the nationals, but I had done my very best and felt so happy with the results of my work.

So many people came up to me to encourage me and compliment my sound and technique and to ask my age. I was almost three years younger than any other player and it was my first competition!

My dream is to play the great concertos with orchestras. The process and exposure of competing has helped many older players and attracted the attention of conductors.

Even though "everyone loves a winner," learning to compete with yourself makes you grow so fast in terms of your playing, especially at 12. I'm really proud for learning so much and making it all the way to nationals in my first competition; it makes me smile during practice and helps to keep me going—and when you think about it, that's pretty cool.

Next up, three competitions to play with orchestras this summer . . . . I'll let you know how I do and what I learn.

DID YOU KNOW?

Before TONY HAWK became an internationally known competitive skateboarder, a savvy businessman who owns a successful clothing and skate-gear company, and the host of *Tony Hawk's Demolition Radio* show, before he even learned how to grind on a half pipe, he played the violin.

A couple of years ago he told a fan on his website chat room that playing a stringed instrument is the No. 1 thing he wanted to do as a hobby. He later told *Teen Ink* magazine that he has purchased a new violin and is planning to get back into it.

"I miss the violin, actually," the skateboard king told *Teen Ink*. "I literally did give it up for skating, because I felt I could only have one extracurricular activity, and I felt my skating was improving faster than my violin skills. But I just recently got a new violin, so I'm going to try to take it up again. Might be a little late, but still fun."

By the way, it was Linnea Brophy of Tennessee who won first place in the 2006 MTNA National Junior String Division and hopefully she will come to New York and stay with us for a visit.

Making a new musical friend is just another plus to the whole experience.

Sarah-Hadley Yakir, 12, studies violin with Grigory Kalinovsky at the Manhattan School of Music, where she also studies theory, ear training, chamber, orchestra, composition, and conducting. For information on entering the MTNA National Student Competitions, visit www.mtna.org.

TAKE CARE
OF YOURSELF

I need something for my excitement, my joy, my tears, and my anger. The violin acts as a sponge for the negatives, soaking them out, and as a megaphone for the positives, amplifying them to the world. The most important thing I've ever been told was when my teacher, Dr. Jerrie Lucktenberg, pointed at my stand and said, "That is not music." Then she pointed at my violin in my hands and said, "That is."

— Caroline, 16, violin

CHAPTER 6

STAYING HEALTHY

Nurturing adolescent wellness isn't such a stretch

By James Reel

You're young. You're indestructible. You're a musician. You're not going to get hurt practicing. It's not as if you were playing football. Oh, sure, maybe you've heard older professional musicians complaining about pain, numbness, inflammation, and muscle spasms. Recently, for example, members of the Boston Symphony Orchestra were hurting so much that they asked their music director, James Levine, to ease up on the rehearsal schedule and to program shorter concerts.

But those are people who've been playing for decades. You're basically just getting started. You're invincible, right?

Wrong. You're never too young to get hurt. Forty to 60 percent of music students report suffering some sort of pain or injury. One study found that the chief physical complaints of music students arose from overuse (as you become more fatigued, you lose some of your sense of pain, which is not good) and tension. Behind these was a general lack of physical conditioning.

Lisa Britsch has seen it happen for years. Back when she was teaching high-school orchestra, she had one student who would come in every Tuesday and say, "I can't play. It hurts ever since I played in youth symphony last night."

Britsch was puzzled. "I knew the youth symphony director, and he didn't let kids play in pain," she says. "There had to be something else going on."

> **Playing in pain is not OK. If something hurts, something's wrong.**
> —Lisa Britsch

That student inspired Britsch to look into ways to help teen musicians avoid chronic pain, or at least get help for it. She decided to pursue graduate studies in the music-education program at Michigan State University. "Playing in pain is not OK," she warns. "If something hurts, something's wrong."

Have Healthy Habits

Britsch says that one big cause of trouble is failing to warm up properly before practice or performance. Another, especially among college students, is practicing too much. "Injuries happen when there's a sudden increase of practice. Students don't work their way into it and [instead] just plunge into practice before a recital," she says.

Britsch says that many music teachers who've never dealt with pain themselves aren't sure how to spot problems in their students and offer help. One teacher who definitely is up on the subject is Judith Palac, one of Britsch's professors at Michigan State University. Healthy music habits have become one of her specialties.

"The first thing you have to do to avoid injury," Palac says, "is develop healthy habits overall. Some musical kids tend to be bookish and don't get out and do sports, but sports can be great for musicians.

"Swimming is best, because it's not only a cardiovascular exercise, it also increases strength and flexibility by stretching. It's also a tension reducer, and it's about the least dangerous sport. You can't really hurt yourself swimming, unless you drown."

Palac says you don't have to get involved in the usual jock activities if you don't want to. "Fencing, ballroom dancing, anything that gets the heart rate up and gets you toned up is helpful," she says. Avoid volleyball, though; that's dangerous to the

fingers. Weight lifting isn't the best idea, either, she says, especially if it's done for body building rather than general toning.

"Weight lifting for body building shortens and thickens the
muscle fibers," she points out. "For music making, you want muscle fibers to lengthen, to support better movement and increase
flexibility."

Watch Your Posture

When it comes time to practice or perform, one of the most important things to think about is posture. "Posture isn't just standing
up straight," says Palac. "It's more like dynamic balance, and teens
don't have it. Their legs grow faster than their arms, and their trunk
muscles are the last to develop, so they have less trunk strength.
Very often they're hunched over. The best way to contend with this
is to be very conscious of your posture every time you work with
your instrument. Before you pick up that violin or cello, though,
you need to warm up and stretch, which are two different things.

6 Before you pick up that
violin or cello, you need
to warm up and stretch.9
—Judith Palac

"With my students," says Palac, "we warm up every day by
doing the hokey-pokey or walking in a circle or something that
will get the blood flowing and warm up the muscles away from

the instrument. If you're starting cold, you need to warm up before you stretch. Then stretch for a few minutes before rehearsal, and you should also stretch a little in the middle or at the end of rehearsal, because muscle fibers shorten up and get thicker when they're fatigued; if we stretch them out at the end of rehearsal, they'll be less likely to cramp the next day."

Palac and string teacher Lisa Britsch know perfectly well that you might think this is burdensome, tedious, or terminally uncool. But paying attention to techniques that will keep you from getting injured will pay off, and not just in music.

Smooth and Easy

OK, so you're ready to sit down and play. You've warmed up and you're thinking about your posture. You have your instrument and bow in hand. Now what?

"First, move smoothly," Palac advises. "When you throw a baseball, you wind up, then throw, and then follow through. When you play an instrument, you have to maintain good movement patterns and think about preparation; if you don't you can injure your muscles and soft tissues and joints.

"Then there's leverage. Use as much muscular force as necessary, but as little as possible. Some kids get into pushing down on the string and pushing down on the bow rather than using muscles to produce weight, not force. And never pound your fingers on the fingerboard.

"Stay in the middle range of motion, which is the healthiest place for every joint," Palac continues. "That means the wrist is practically straight out from the arm, not bent too much. You should play so your body looks like arcs and spirals, not squares and trapezoids.

"Balance. Spread your weight evenly across the base of your body, whether you're sitting or standing. And don't hike one shoulder higher than the other. Since we all go forward all the time in string playing, because we're reaching around something, it's good to stretch your arms and back backward when you're finished playing to counteract that forward motion."

The Right Stuff

Developing basic healthy habits is often enough to avoid major problems. During practice, manage your workload by taking breaks. Palac recommends at least standing and bending back for 20 seconds every half hour; if your practice lasts longer than an hour, it's good to take a ten-minute break for every hour of work. "This seems like a lot to think about," says Palac, "but if we start out this way, pretty soon it becomes part of our natural routine."

Then there's the question of having the right stuff. Like the right kind of chair. It should be tall enough that your upper legs are parallel to the ground with your lower legs aiming for the floor at a 90-degree angle. You most certainly shouldn't sit with your knees above your hip joints.

And don't forget the stuff that attaches to your instrument. "A lot of students get tired of looking for the right fit and just try to conform their bodies to their instrument rather than the other way around," says Palac.

Cellists, for example, may need shorter or longer or even curved endpins for better balance. Violinists and violists need well-fitted chin rests and shoulder rests.

Young students should move on to bigger instruments with caution. "In terms of muscle strain, it's better for the instrument to be a little small than too large," says Palac.

Let the Spirit Move You

Bodywork practices, such as the Alexander Technique and the Feldenkrais Method, are used by many musicians—and athletes—to improve body and mind.

The Alexander Technique was developed by Frederick Matthias Alexander. The technique reeducates muscles by teaching players to rethink how they move, which, in most cases, means

WISE WORDS

Playing the violin has been my tool for examining every principle in life that I have been exposed to or enlightened by. The skills of discipline, awareness, and concentration that one acquires from studying the violin far outweigh the musical benefits. My love of the violin also led me to the guitar and, later, the mandolin. Something about learning how to deal with one stringed instrument seems to open that door to all of the other ones. It's amazing how you can evoke your entire life's experiences through a piece of vibrating wire and wood.

—*Zach Brock, jazz violinist and bandleader*

breaking all those nasty habits that result in unbearably knotted neck, shoulder, and back muscles.

To find an Alexander Technique practitioner in your area, visit www.alexandertechnique.com/teacher.

The Feldenkrais Method is another favored treatment for string players. Dr. Moshe Feldenkrais developed this course of study that centers on the use of gentle, subtle movements to enhance the body's efficiency and grace.

Visit www.feldenkrais.com for info.

Yoga and Pilates classes also can help string players increase their body awareness. These practices are incredibly popular and are widely offered at health clubs and private studios throughout the world.

"Alexander Technique people and Pilates teachers are good with the mechanics of the human body," says Palac. "They can help you use your body better so you don't get injured again."

Take Your Medicine

If you do develop pain, don't panic. Sometimes a new playing technique will cause temporary aches. But if the pain persists, talk to your teacher. Rest more, and stop playing when it hurts. There's disagreement over whether to apply ice or heat to the problem area, but Palac says, "Ice for ten minutes to an hour can't hurt you."

Go to your doctor, and explain exactly where it hurts and what you're doing when the pain starts. He or she may not be completely familiar with the injuries that arise from playing, so you may need to visit a specialist in performing-arts medicine, or, if that's too far away, a good sports-medicine doctor. (This may cost more than seeing a general physician, but your problem will likely be solved in only one or two visits.)

Do what the doctor tells you to do.

If you're supposed to take an anti-inflammatory for two weeks, do it for the entire two weeks; don't stop early, because even if the pain is gone the underlying inflammation may not yet be completely eliminated.

Former Teen Strings *associate editor Tiffany Martini contributed to this article.*

CHAPTER 7

STRESSED FOR SUCCESS

*Make stage fright and audition anxiety
work for—not against— you*

By David Templeton

Imagine the worst audition you could ever experience. Picture a stifling, noisy, overcrowded waiting room with a malfunctioning air conditioner, with you and dozens of other perspiring musicians waiting interminably before being called out to the stage—where matters grow even worse. You can't find your violin. The sheet music is gone. The music stand keeps falling over. And once you finally start playing, the stage lights suddenly go out, plunging you into blackness at the precise moment that somebody drops a huge hunk of lumber onto the stage—right behind you—with a deafening crash.

Bad, huh? Enough to drive a person screaming out the door, or, at the very least, to cause a good, solid player to melt down mid-audition. Right? Actually, wrong, according to Dr. Don Greene, who believes that stress, when properly prepared for, can actually be good for a musician.

A trained sports and performance psychologist, Greene has for several years been developing specific coping methods for classical musicians—both students and professionals—who sometimes suffer from performance anxiety or who simply fall apart in high-stress situations. The trick, he says, is not to try to control or minimize the level of stress, but to welcome it, to count on it, and even—with a little practice—to make use of it.

> 6When practicing, you want to apply more pressure, more adversity, than might happen in the actual game.9
> —Don Greene

"One of the biggest mistakes a performer makes is to assume that performance anxiety is abnormal, that it's bad," explains Greene. "It's not good or bad—it's just adrenaline." In short: Stop fearing fear.

"The principle of sports psychology is overcompensation," says Greene. "When practicing, you want to apply more pressure, more adversity than might happen in the actual game or performance. So then, when all that stress and pressure does happen, you can say, 'Well, I've dealt with a lot worse than this. I can do this—no problem.'"

Here are a few tips for understanding and using stress and anxiety to your advantage:

Train Your Brain

According to Greene, musicians who don't do well under stress end up looking for solutions in technical things, energetically sharpening their musical skills while ignoring the actual problem. "If you can do a piece in a practice room—efficiently and well—then you have the technical abilities to do it," he says. "But then if you go on stage and are not able to execute the piece, it's not a technical issue. It's a mental issue, an issue of how you deal with stress. A lot of people then will go back to the practice room to work on a problem that wasn't there, namely their technique, when the

DID YOU KNOW?

You might know actor KIEFER SUTHERLAND for his role as anti-terrorist agent Jack Bauer from the action-packed hit TV series *24*. But did you know that Sutherland began studying violin at age four and landed his first big acting role as a result? Yup, his break-through Los Angeles stage role at age 11 was in *Throne of Straw*, which required an actor who could play a violin solo in the second act. You just never know how those violin lessons might pay off.

problem wasn't their technique—it was their response to stress.

"The problem is not their bowing—it's their bowing under pressure."

Practice Performing

When musicians practice, Greene has observed, they are rehearsing more than just their musical skills. "Classical musicians are used to spending a massive amount of time—and rightfully so—in practicing, doing all the things in practice they need to do," Greene observes, "stopping, checking, correcting, trying a different way of fingering, a different method of bowing, playing pieces in fits and starts, doing all the things a student, and even a professional, needs to do to get the technical piece of the repertoire down.

"The mistake I see is that they never switch over from practicing practice to practicing performance. And then they go out on stage—where the environment is very different—expecting to do something they've never adequately practiced."

How does a performer practice performance?

"I encourage musicians to either play for a friend, a teacher, a colleague, or to simply put a tape recorder on or set up a video camera," Greene says. "Having a person there or a camera or a tape recorder puts pressure on you, and you realize that, and that's beautiful, because then you're practicing performing."

The whole idea is to apply as much stress as possible, so that it mimics, as closely as possible, the conditions of being in a performance. "Believe me," he laughs "it's better that you figure out how to deal with the stress and find good ways among friends than to wait and see what happens in front of an audition panel, a jury, or a paying audience at a professional gig."

Fake It

While Greene encourages his musicians to practice making their entrances and exits—since an entrance can be a powerful anxiety trigger for certain performers—there's more to it than merely walking onto the stage and standing there. "When a lot of people step out on stage, their adrenaline is pumping," he says. "So when my musicians practice performance, I want them going up and down stairs or doing jumping jacks or something before they practice making their entrance. That way, they can feel some of the symptoms of what they may feel when they actually are making an entrance in front of an audience."

Whatever you do—don't relax!

"Powerful performance is not about being relaxed," suggests Dr. Greene. "You have to accept that when you perform, you might be feeling some extra energy, and the more you can get used to feeling that energy when you play your first few notes, the better."

Don Greene is the author of Fight Your Fear . . . and Win: 7 Skills for Performing Your Best Under Pressure; Performance Success: Performing Your Best Under Pressure; *and* Audition Success: An Olympic Sports Psychologist Teaches Performing Artists How to Win.

GET AHEAD

Playing the bass has served as the best form of communication for me. The only time I ever really opened up was in my poetry, but everyone doesn't understand the concepts of poetry easily. So something else was needed. Then I came across the bass and, through music, was able to speak volumes. Some argue that the bass, with its intimidating size and thick strings, is one of the more difficult instruments to learn. By conquering this challenge, I have been endowed with the courage to move head-on with all other challenges I find myself facing.

—*Markell, 19, double bass*

CHAPTER 8

YOUR PARENTS, YOUR PALS

5 ways your parents can support your musical journey

By Donna Shryer

Do you ever feel as though playing that stringed instrument is a chore? Are you bored with all the scales, note reading, and practicing? Every musician, beginner as well as advanced, feels this way sometimes. The good news is that you can work through these temporary feelings and refresh your musical enthusiasm. Buddying up with your parents is a smart place to begin. As a team, you'll boost music's fun factor, and as we all know, having a great time is the best motivator around.

Here are five ways that young musicians—just like you—share their musical journey with mom and pop.

1. The Mix Master

When 11-year-old Anna Cieslik, from Chicago, Illinois, feels herself losing interest in violin, she mixes in new music for motivation. "First I go out to lunch with Dad and then we go buy a new CD. I get to pick whatever I want as long as someone on the CD plays violin," she explains. "Afterwards we come home and listen to the

CD, sometimes I go online and read about the violin player. I find out lots of cool stuff. Did you know that Martie Maguire, from the Dixie Chicks, learned with the Suzuki method? That's how I'm learning.

"How cool is that?"

During her three years as a violin student, Anna has collected quite a CD assortment. So, when she needs motivation, she puts aside Bach, Beethoven, and Mozart and instead does homework to the electrifying sounds of Bond, eats dinner to the Dixie Chicks, and Afro-Cuban jazz violinist Susie Hansen gives dessert a hot Latin flavor.

Mom likes to point out that many of Anna's favorite string players are not only talented but also just as glamorous as some other celebrities on the pop-music charts.

Invite your parents on a CD shopping adventure! Here's a list of inspirational string players to get you started: Bond (rock/pop); Dixie Chicks (neotraditionalist country, country-pop, contemporary country); Elana James and the Hot Club of Cow Town (western-swing revivalists); Lili Haydn (rock/pop); Susie Hansen (Latin jazz, salsa); Ashley MacIsaac (Celtic punk, post-grunge); Natalie MacMaster (Celtic folk, traditional and contemporary); Ruth Ungar and the Mammals (pop-folk); and Sara Watkins and Nickel Creek (bluegrass).

2. Step Out of Your Style

Some young string players find inspiration by taking a lesson or two from somebody who teaches in a very different style from their usual instructor. It doesn't even have to be a formal lesson. A few hours of coaching often motivates great things!

Here's how it works. If, for example, your studies revolve around classical music, ask your parents to help you locate someone in town who teaches with a Celtic, jazz, rock, or Cajun spin. If you and your parents enjoyed a local performer at a music festival or coffee house, give this person a call and ask if he or she'd mentor you for a few hours.

Jessica Baron Turner, a California-based music teacher and author of *Your Musical Child: Inspiring Kids to Play and Sing for Keeps* (www.strings-magazine.com), says this trick is sure to fire up your energy level. She adds, "What's important is that you and this person take a piece you

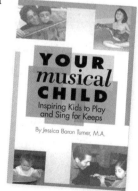

know very well—something that's really boring to you—and then completely rearrange it in this coach's particular style.

"Bravely rearrange it!

"You can totally amuse yourself, and something you once found very dreary will suddenly be so exciting."

3. Playing Around

A quick way to climb out of a musical rut is to play your violin during an after-school activity that's unrelated to weekly lessons. That's what ten-year-old Chicagoan Sasha Simon did. He tried out for his school play and earned a small part, but when the show's director heard that Sasha plays violin, he was asked to perform three fiddle songs onstage. It was a perfect fit, since the play had a country/western theme.

As Sasha puts it, "I'm so happy I had a better part in the show, and it's all because I study violin. I didn't know it's so much fun to show people what I've been working on all these years. And now I look forward to practicing at home, so I have more to show people."

What are some other new and exciting ways to use your violin? Well, many schools have a band, which by definition does not include stringed instruments, but if Mom or Dad contacts the band instructor, an exception is often possible. You would play either the flute or oboe parts on your stringed instrument. Your parents might also contact your school's choir director. A pianist or acoustic guitarist often accompanies vocal groups, but a violinist might be a terrific change of pace for both you and the choir members.

4. Applause, Applause

Robin Kearton directs World-on-a-String, a string camp in Champaign, Illinois, and she also leads a group of young violinists called the Bow-Dacious String Band. Robin feels there's nothing like a performance to get the mojo going and, she adds, it's easy to start your own group.

"First grab two or three musicians at your same level. This can include all violinists or you could invite someone who plays keyboard and another person who plays guitar. Next think of a great name for your group. Once you have a small repertoire, find a place to play!"

Here's where your parents can help. While many establishments welcome offers to play, it is often required that an adult be officially in charge. Check out shopping centers, public libraries, local art festivals, and retirement communities. Then there's also busking: performing in public while listeners toss money into your open violin case. Kearton's group often does this, and then the Bow-Dacious String Band donates the money to a local charity, like the Humane Society.

Before busking, always contact the property owner or manager and ask permission. Some cities have ordinances against it. Robin says that a great busking location is your local farmers' market.

WISE WORDS

The best part of playing in any band is actually playing with other people. It's the camaraderie. Being able to bounce ideas off of and critiquing each other's playing has helped me tremendously as a bass player.

—*Chris Maas, psychobilly bassist of the Phenomenauts*

55

5. Take It from the Top

If listening to adult string players doesn't get you motivated then spend time with kids your own age. There's a terrific weekly radio show, distributed by Public Radio International, that gives you just such an opportunity. It's called *From the Top* (hosted by Christopher O'Riley, a pianist who has released two popular CDs of Radiohead transcriptions), and each show features young musicians, ages nine to 18. The musicians not only perform but also answer lots of questions, including how to stay focused and motivated.

The three violin-playing Lamb sisters, Karis, 17, Kiemel, 15, and Kolson, 13, from Tuscaloosa, Alabama, performed earlier this year on *From the Top* and Karis describes the experience as unlike any other. "Just to see young people my own age who exemplify such incredibly focused passion and focused diligence to their instrument . . . that just creates a whole new desire," she says, "a whole new energy to push my own goals even further."

Not every young string player can perform on *From the Top*, but you can get involved in local contests through your school or community. Your parents can help you search for opportunities. If you're interested in auditioning for the show, log onto www.fromthetop.org. There you'll find show schedules, a station in your area that carries the show, interviews with previously featured young performers, an opportunity to hear performance pieces, and instructions to audition.

Good luck, and keep practicing—and remember, your parents are your pals and can help you stay motivated in exciting ways.

CHAPTER 9

HIGH SCHOOL CONFIDENTIAL

*Prepping for a music-school audition can be stressful.
These tips can help you breeze through the process*

By Donna Shryer

To study music at the university, college, or conservatory level, your admission depends in part on an audition. And to prepare for that, you'll want to start getting ready during your sophomore year of high school. Before outlining what you need to compete, here's some wise advice, courtesy of Mimi Zweig, professor of violin at Indiana University Jacobs School of Music and also a member of the school's audition committee.

1. Select a repertoire within your skill range, so you play beautifully from beginning to end. Audition committees do not expect you to know everything—teaching you everything is the school's job.

2. Practice your repertoire so it becomes second nature. Ignoring point No. 1, Zweig says, is the most common mistake students make, and it can prevent you from achieving point No. 2. "We often accept a young person who shows a lot of potential, but maybe hasn't had the opportunity to develop that potential," Zweig says. "We're looking for students who show aptitude and are dedicated to learning.

> *selecting music outside your reach is asking for disaster.*
> —Stacia Spencer

"Be sure you select a repertoire you can achieve. And don't worry. The audition committee is trained to hear your potential."

Stacia Spencer, senior lecturer in string pedagogy at Northwestern School of Music and a private teacher experienced in helping students prepare their audition repertoire, agrees completely. "Selecting music outside your reach is asking for disaster," she says.

"This is not the time to show off. Trust me, if you play something beyond your true capabilities, the audition team will only hear mistakes. On the other hand, if you select an easier piece but something you play beautifully, the audition team will only hear your terrific vibrato, your musicality, and your skill. Then the committee members begin thinking about where they can take you . . . as their student. This is a good place to be.

"It's where you want to be!"

Where to Start

Now that you know you're under no pressure to wow the audition-committee members off their chairs with the difficulty of your selections, here's some practical advice for creating an audition-worthy winning repertoire. Begin by phoning, contacting online, or visiting, if possible, all of your target schools' admissions offices. You want to do this around 18 months before the actual audition, which gives you six months to research schools and one year to prepare your audition repertoire. You'll find that audition requirements vary and—more important—that admission into a college or university music school is often a two-tiered process, involving both the school's overall admission requirements as well as the music school's requirements. This means high-school grades and SAT scores come into play, and musical ability alone won't get you in.

Generally speaking, at your audition you'll be required to play one movement from a major concerto, or sometimes two contrasting movements, as well as two unaccompanied Bach movements. Some schools require an etude of the student's choosing and, on occasion, scales. In addition, a music school may require prospective students to take a written test involving music theory. These tests, however, are often used more for placement than as a basis for acceptance.

You may also need to submit a recording of your playing—a CD, tape, or DVD—as part of your admission process. These recordings are used to prescreen applicants, and if the audition committee approves, you are then invited to audition. This does not need to be a professional recording or involve great expense, but it should accurately represent your playing. These screening recordings come with their own set of deadlines, which is another reason to phone your chosen schools' admissions offices or go online to read the schools' audition and interview requirements.

Once you've figured out the requirements, the next step is to discuss repertoire options with your music teacher, preferably one year before auditioning. This, Spencer stresses, allows for plenty of practice and performance time, and even the luxury of putting the music aside, taking a brief head-clearing break, and then coming back to it. Getting an early start on your repertoire also means you have time to try out different pieces and eventually settle on the right music

DID YOU KNOW?

Cello ensembles come in all sizes. From the solo inventions of pop cellist LINDSAY MAC to the Metallica-infused mania of the Finnish foursome APOCALYPTICA to the 12 CELLISTS OF THE BERLIN PHILHARMONIC, cellists around the globe are finding new and creative ways to make their mark on the string world.

for your ability level—so that during the audition you can play it beautifully from beginning to end.

Sharpen Your Stage Presence

To really nail that audition, students ought to get up in front of the committee with tons of performance time behind them. "They should be doing this repertoire for the 100th time," Zweig suggests. "Stage presence is important, and you want to present yourself in a professional manner. You may think you're auditioning to be a music student, but the committee often thinks on a grander scale— you're auditioning to be a performer.

"That's what we are: performers!"

Master classes, summer camp, quartets, high school orchestra—they're all means to sharpen your stage presence. As for your specific repertoire, you want to play it again and again for fellow musicians, parents, grandparents, and any one else you can grab.

"An audition is the tip of the iceberg," Zweig says. "Preparation is the key to success. These auditions are only 10 to 15 minutes long. There's no time to warm up and shake off nerves. You need to be completely comfortable in front of an audience."

One thing that you probably do not want to do, Spencer advises, is to change teachers solely because he or she has a high ratio of students accepted into respected music schools. It's an increasingly common idea, in light of the ever-growing emphasis on SAT coaches and ghostwriters for college application essays. "If you're happy with your teacher, you're learning all the technical aspects—scales and etudes—and you're happy with your playing, absolutely do not seek out another teacher," she says. "You can definitely get outside guidance in master classes or summer camp, but to go and study with another teacher one year before you audition is not good. Every teacher is different, and you'll hear conflicting advice. Then all you have is confusion—and big problems."

To really nail that audition, students want to get up in front of the committee with tons of performance time behind them.

So, how do you know if you have the right teacher? Zweig says it's as simple as listening to yourself play. "If you sound beautiful then you're getting the right information. Experience on the teacher's part is not necessarily important."

This brings us back to where we began. Your goal is to play beautifully before the audition committee. To achieve this, set realistic goals and always remember—this is an audition to learn. If the committee chose only those who know it all, the members would be out of a job!

BE PREPARED

Here are **10 tips** on getting ready for a successful college audition:

Research school admission and audition requirements, and that means every school on your hit list. You can count on an audition, as well as variables.

Evaluate repertoire selections with your teacher. This person knows your capabilities and will help you choose pieces that show off your potential without going beyond it.

Practice the music, but also practice auditioning, sometimes called "mock auditions." Perform for friends, teachers, family, and anyone else who will listen.

Expression is as important as technical skill. As you practice, give both elements equal attention.

Review the basics, like music theory, ear training, and keyboard skills. Even if there's no test requirement, you'll be able to confidently converse with the audition committee.

Take every piece apart and be ready to begin playing at any point. The audition committee may ask you to repeat a small phrase.

Own your progress. Take master classes, play with a quartet, attend summer camp—any opportunity to sharpen your stage presence.

Impressions count. You want to stand in front of the audition committee looking like a confident performer!

Record your program—on a CD, tape, or DVD—to either send before the audition or leave behind. If no recording is required, use it to assess your playing.

Enjoy yourself! From selecting to practicing to performing your repertoire, have fun. The audition committee is looking for a passionate musician—not someone who knows it all.

—D.S.

CHAPTER 10

WISH YOU WERE HERE

4 questions to ask before picking
the perfect summer string camp

By Donna Shryer

There's an old Swedish proverb: A life without love is like a year without summer. Find the right summer music camp, and you may be tempted to flip the phrase: A life without summer camp is a year without love.

"Summer music camp is the best place to fall in love," says Jon Feller, Chicago-based violin instructor, founder of the Andersonville Suzuki Academy, and faculty member at the Bow-Dacious String Band Summer Camp in Urbana-Champaign, Illinois. He is referring, of course, to a love affair with music and the thrill of making it.

"You'll experience musical possibilities you never knew existed," he adds. "It's so invigorating to be with all these like-minded people. There's a sensitivity between musicians and this connection often turns into lifelong friendships. Really, the best times I ever had were at music camp."

> **The best times I ever had were at music camp.**
> —Jon Feller

Fortunately for string players, summer camp is a broad term encompassing a diverse range of skill levels, intensity, music styles, and time commitments, so you can be sure there's a camp for you! One thing, however, remains constant from camp to camp—they all provide a memorable experience that's sure to energize your relationship to music.

With so many music-camp options, selecting the perfect warm-weather experience can be confusing. Here are four questions that will help you narrow the playing field.

1. Am I a serious musician who wants to make a ton of progress this summer?

This is the big one, explains Ronda Cole, internationally renowned violin teacher, head of the Suzuki Violin Program at the University of Maryland School of Music, and director of the Suzuki Summer Institute for children and parents, Washington, D.C. "You need to ask yourself, 'Do I expect to come out of this as a better-developed player or do I want a range of activities that includes music?' If you're serious about advancing your skills, then you want a camp where you practice your brains out and really end up in a higher place. You can accomplish a year's worth of progress in one summer because you don't have to deal with other things. You're not exhausted, over-scheduled, and concerned about homework."

Cole suggests that anyone seeking this "higher place" should consider camps that include at least three to four hours a day for practice. These camps are often geared toward musicians seriously considering a career in music, or at least someone who's been bitten by the music bug and already practices many hours a day. "This person knows where he or she wants to go and summer camp is one more step toward that goal," Cole says.

If this sounds like the sort of camp for you, but you can't decide between options, then consider the camp faculty. For instance, if you're interested in studying with a specific professor

WISE WORDS

How did I know string playing was something I wanted to do? It was a part of my life from such an early age [age four] that it's like asking, 'How did you know when you liked speaking English?' I never questioned it and I never wanted to quit. When I got to be 11 years old, music started to mean even more to me. It became an emotional thing rather than something I just did. That year, at summer camp after lights were out, I'd listen to a recording of Heifetz playing the Wieniawski D minor concerto. It gave me goose bumps.'

—Joshua Bell, violinist

at a particular college or university, find out if this professor is on staff at a camp.

If so, then you've solved the dilemma.

2. Am I dedicated to my instrument and want inspiration along with camaraderie?

If you love music, love playing music, and love talking about music with other musicians, but don't see a career in music, then look for a camp with a diverse schedule of music-related activities. Some

camps offer lessons along with opportunities to participate in quartets, orchestras, jazz ensembles, chamber groups, choirs, and sometimes even rock 'n' roll bands. Students play violin all day, but they don't spend a lot of time practicing. As Feller puts it, "The idea here is to expand your horizons. Not only music, but also artistic, creative, and social horizons."

While this sort of camp might frustrate the career-minded musician, it's not fluff. "Spending time within a society of string players validates so much of what you're doing at home!" Feller explains. "A light goes on. 'Oh, this is why I do it—to make music with other people.'

"Camps are often a wake-up experience."

3. Do I love swimming as much as music, art as much as viola?

A third type of summer music camp combines the traditional camp agenda with music.

In addition to lessons, there's ample time for swimming, crafts, baseball, and all the other summer activities. This, Cole suggests, is a solid option for any musician who enjoys music along with everything else. "At this sort of camp you're playing your instrument one minute and then it's off to the pool to get your lifeguard badge."

These camps often provide opportunities to try different instruments. Generally speaking, you bring your own instrument

SURVIVAL KIT

Finding the right camp is your first challenge in planning the perfect summer-study experience. The second? Deciding what to pack! As camps are held anywhere from the middle of a redwood grove to the middle of a teacher's living room, your needs will obviously depend heavily on your chosen setting. There are a few items, however, that should make an appearance in any music-student's suitcase this summer.

1. Pencils and a big eraser for marking music.
2. Extra strings. Just in case!
3. A recorder and extra batteries for lessons and master classes.
4. A stand light that can double as a book light.
5. Good summer reading. Check out ARNOLD STEINHARDT's book *Violin Dreams* about his life as a musician.

for planned instruction but then break off into groups with fellow campers—where you can experiment with drums, piano, guitar, or whatever other instrument you have an itch to play!

4. Am I a fiddler at heart?

The fourth type of summer program involves a specialty camp—fiddle, jazz, improvisation, chamber music, etc. It's a chance to experience different teaching techniques, play different music, and break out of routine. And it's a great opportunity to fine-tune skills for that garage band back home or to prepare for busking—performing in public places as passersby toss money into a container, usually an open instrument case. But it also can lead to a professional career.

Natalie Haas, a recent Juilliard grad and member of the Appalachia Waltz Trio, honed her Scottish cello skills at the Valley of the Moon Scottish Fiddling School summer camp beneath sun-dappled redwoods along California's central coast.

After asking—and answering—these four questions, the next step is to talk with your music teacher. This person knows your skill and comfort level, and should have suggestions about which type of camp experience is best for you.

As for camp preparation, let's return to those four questions for a moment. If you answered yes to either question one or two, then the camp for you may require an audition. This should not be stressful, though. As Jon Feller says, "If you're studying privately, then you're used to recitals and you should have something recital-ready or nearly so. Like any solo performance, you need to prepare, but unless you're at a very elite level, you would prepare as you would for any performance."

Just remember: all these camps are fun. It's just that fun means something different to the career-development camper than it does to someone who's interested in music along with many other summer activities. So it's important to find the right camp.

But, says Ronda Cole, it's effort well spent. "Summer music camp should be a part of every musician's normal routine. It lets you know that the world of music is a whole lot bigger than a weekly lesson and practicing in the bedroom.

"I consider it core education!"

SEEK AND FIND

Need more help finding the right camp? Visit our searchable online Summer Study Guide at www.teenstrings.com. Here you can search by program type, geographical location, or specific program name to get a list of

pertinent options with basic information for each camp, including contact information and, if available, a link to each camp's website.

GET IN GEAR

I like my cello most likely more than I do any person in my life. It gives me a place to go where I can connect with myself, and not have to worry about people thinking about me, or anything else. It's just me and the cello, and I like that.

— Ann, 13, cello

CHAPTER 11

STEPPING UP

Time for a new axe?
Here's how to find a step-up instrument
to fit your needs.

By Sarah Freiberg

When you began to play a stringed instrument, you probably purchased an inexpensive start-up instrument or even rented your first one. You (or your parents) may not have been sure whether you'd like it, or whether you were ready to take care of it. If you were very young, you may have chosen a fractional size, and you probably outgrew that instrument in no time at all. The advantage to renting was that you could trade in the instrument for the next size up—or a better-quality model—and it would be insured in case of accidents.

But now that you've been practicing diligently for all those years and have become more responsible, you may be ready to graduate to a bigger and better instrument that will help you develop as a musician. It's time to acquire your very own violin, viola, cello, or bass—your first "step-up" instrument.

A step-up instrument can be defined simply as a better-quality, better-sounding axe, most likely crafted by a contemporary maker or workshop (and usually with a better resale value).

Here are a few things to consider:

Where to Begin

Ask your teacher for recommendations. He or she probably has helped many students find their first instrument. It may well be that the shop you rent from sells instruments as well. While some shops have a rent-to-own policy, you shouldn't plan to buy the instrument you've been renting unless you absolutely love it and can't imagine a better one. Yanbing Chen, co-owner of Goronok String Instruments in Cleveland, suggests that the buyer beware: "One thing to watch out for is that some music stores will lock you in to the instrument you are renting. That's not good."

These aren't always the best-quality instruments, he adds, and may not be in pristine condition—a series of renters can be hard on an instrument. On the other hand, many string shops have a policy that lets you apply a percentage of the rental fee toward the purchase of another instrument—after you've been renting for a predetermined amount of time.

What to Ask

Susan Horkan, former sales manager for Johnson String Instrument in Newton Center, Massachusetts, notes, "Most prospective buyers don't have a lot of information about purchasing instruments, and there really isn't much out there," but she does feel that it's helpful to know the structural parts of the instrument. Also, find out the condition of the instruments that you are looking at—particularly the antiques. The health of an instrument is crucial. If the instrument is new, research the maker or the company that made it. Horkan considers her role as seller to include educating prospective buyers in what to look for: the types of instruments available in their price range; the pros and cons of contemporary and antique instruments; and the types of sound available.

WISE WORDS

The first time I played, it was a revelation because the cello allowed me to express my emotional range with its two extremes. The cello gives me the variety of colors I need to draw my musical painting.

—*Jorane (aka Joanne Pelletier),*
cellist

The *British Rough Guide* book series (www.roughguides.com) is a good place to start—and at a very good price. You're about to make a significant purchase, so it's wise to know as much as you can. The company publishes the *Rough Guide to Violin & Viola* as well as the *Rough Guide to Cello*, both of which offer plenty of helpful tips.

How Much Will It Cost?

Prices of contemporary step-up instruments range from $1,500 to $5,000; an antique instrument could cost much more. Although you may think that a higher price means a better instrument, sometimes a premium is attached for details such as fancier fittings, more intricate inlay, and other niceties that don't necessarily affect the tone of the instrument. There are some very good-quality instruments at the lower end of the spectrum. Define what your upper limit is before you go shopping for your new instrument—and remember there will be plenty to look at throughout each of the price ranges.

Be sure to check the Violin Pricing Guide in the 2007 *Strings* Buyer's Guide for contact and pricing information on numerous makers and their going rates. (The guide is available online at www.stringsmagazine.com.) Many musicians even have had custom instruments made within these low- to mid-range prices. The good news is, as Horkan puts it, "There are so many great contemporary makers [and] terrific new instruments that are reliable, consistent, and structurally sound."

Set Your Standards

Choosing an instrument is a very personal endeavor, and it takes time. Make sure to allot an hour or two when you first visit a shop, and don't buy on impulse. Plan to take instruments home to try and play them for your teacher. Visit many shops to compare. Doug Cox, a Vermont-based luthier, says not to worry if the process takes a few months. After all, you're purchasing a fiddle that will be your "voice," one that you will hopefully keep for a long time. Most shops let you take instruments for a week or two for a trial. Try to take home two contrasting instruments so that you can compare them over time.

> Plan to take instruments home and play them for your teacher.

"Although everyone has different tastes," says Horkan, "there are certain things all players can look for in an instrument: responsiveness, ease of playing, evenness of tone from string to string and throughout the range of the instrument. Some players prefer a mellow sound. However, in general I try to steer students toward an open, clean sound.

"Comfort is extremely important. It really works both ways, though: If a student is comfortable with an instrument, he'll pull out a better sound—and if he likes the sound, the instrument feels comfortable."

The Right Fit

Usually, between you and your teacher, you'll know when you have found the right instrument. "In helping a player choose an instru-

INSTRUMENT CARE 101

So, it's time to replace your old strings. Sometimes this simple task can seem overwhelming. Should you remove all the strings at one time? Or should you unwind only one at a time, replacing each one as you go (and if so, where do you start)? "When you need to change an entire set of strings, don't remove all of the old strings at one time—you could lose the correct bridge placement," says Richard Ward of Ifshin Violins in Berkeley, California. "Lack of tension can cause the sound post to fall, something no violinist wants to be faced with."

When changing strings, here's a good guide to follow:

1. Remove one string at a time, starting with the highest or lowest string on your instrument, while keeping the remaining strings up to pitch.

2. Be sure the fine tuner for the string you are about to install is loosened. Drop the ball end of the new string through the fine tuner cartridge. If you don't have fine tuners, thread the string through the string hole in the tailpiece until the ball fastens in place.

3. Thread the first string through the hole in the corresponding peg. Wind the string evenly from the center of the peg to just before the edge of the pegbox. Tighten slowly, tuning while you go. Stop when you fall into the correct tonal range, and use the fine tuner—if applicable—to fine-tune the pitch.

4. Now repeat the process, following the same steps, until all the strings have been replaced. Once you're done, you can get right back to practicing.

—*Heather K. Scott*

ment, I look for verbal and physical cues," Horkan says. "I'm aiming for when a player says, 'I just love this instrument.' Sometimes I can see a player relax with a particular instrument—and I know she's found the right one. Sometimes I may notice students tense up with one instrument and I'll make sure to communicate that to them."

This brings up another issue: standard size of instruments. If you choose a stringed instrument that's a little different (larger or smaller), you'll end up adjusting to it—but it may be hard to readjust when you move on to your next instrument. Cox says that "you become used to a nonstandard instrument—and your technique will end up conforming to it."

Benotti recently went through the process of finding a cello for her son.

They found a particular instrument that had unusually sloping shoulders, she says, but were told by cello colleagues that it would be hard to adjust to, particularly for a child. So they continued their search—ultimately finding just the right one for stepping up.

CHAPTER 12

THE ELECTRIC COMPANY

Learning to handle an electric stringed instrument?
Plug in to new forms of expression

By Erin Shrader

Blaise Kielar of the Electric Violin Shop in Durham, North Carolina, meets a lot of teenagers looking for an electric stringed instrument to take them beyond classical music. And these teens have all kinds of music in mind: playing in jazz ensembles at school, joining the "praise band" at their church, or starting a rock band—all situations in which it can be difficult for an acoustic violin to fit.

The expanded sound capability of an electric stringed instrument can be a powerful creative tool that can keep you engaged and inspired. "I hear about kids who get home with an electric violin and an amp with effects and their parents don't see them for days at a time," laughs Kielar.

83

John Jordan, an electric-violin maker and father of a teenage cellist in Concord, California, agrees. "It's easy to retain string players through middle school, but we start losing them around high school, especially the boys. It becomes perceived as a sissy instrument."

Face it. How cool can you be standing perfectly still, keeping those f-holes pointed at the microphone while everyone else in your band is moving with the groove?

As rock violinist and electric-stringed-instrument manufacturer Mark Wood puts it, "We want to make string players relevant to mainstream music—like we were in the 1800s!"

How It Works

The details can get complicated, but the concepts are simple. String vibrations are turned into an electrical signal by a transducer, better known as a pickup. The signal is carried by a cable to an amplifier that magnifies the strength of the signal enough to move speakers. Speakers vibrate, making the air move in sound waves, which our ears hear.

The term *electric violin* (or viola or cello) actually covers a lot of territory—everything from traditional-looking violins with transducer bridges to solid-body instruments that have no sound

Casey Driessen

84

box at all, with acoustic-electrics in between. Then there are wild instruments like Woods' Viper, shaped like a Flying V with six or seven strings, frets, and a chest support.

Expert Advice

Here's some expert advice for getting an entry-level solid-body electric outfit together:

The expanded sound capability of an electric stringed instrument can be a powerful creative tool.

If your violin shop doesn't do electric, find one that does and establish a relationship. You'll need this dealer for the same things: setup, repairs, and trade-ins. Plus a knowledgeable dealer can help you match gear, which is hugely important.

Start with one that feels like your regular instrument. It can still look cool (how about neon-blue see-through acrylic?), but it may be easier to play if that familiar heel is in the right place, the bridge curve is normal, and your shoulder rest stays on. (The innovative Viper straps on with a shoulder harness.)

"Bad pickups sound cheesy," says Jordan, who suggests starting in the $1,000 range for a decent-sounding, quality instrument. Try out as many electrics as you can to learn the difference. More money generally gets you better sound, plus better workmanship and materials, which can save headaches later on.

Match your gear. Your shop can help you here. Instrument, amplifier, and effects all have to work together and not all combinations work. The details get complicated fast.

Don't get an electric-guitar amp for your violin! Those are designed to make high-pitched guitar solos scream. Check with makers or dealers for amps designed to match the types of pickups used with bowed strings. (Some acoustic-guitar amplifiers fit that bill.) If your fiddle still sounds crunchy through a good amp, you may need a preamp, which raises the signal before it reaches the main amp, smoothing out the sound.

> ## WISE WORDS
>
> **Being able to master any technique is an accomplishment, but being able to make music brings the most satisfaction.**
>
> —*Eric Gorfain of rock group the Section Quartet*

Jordan is impressed with the number of quality practice amps available in the $100–$150 range. More power and better-quality speakers start at about $500. If you will be plugging into a PA system, make sure that running a line from the amp to the board doesn't disconnect your amp's speaker. This happens with some lower-end amps.

Sonic Sojourn

The fun of going electric is exploring sounds that no acoustic instrument ever made. Effects processors are designed to manipulate the signal, changing the sound. Jordan suggests starting with a multieffects box. For "way less than $100," you can get multieffects boxes that feature reverb, delay, chorus, and wah-wah. As you learn which effects you like best and how to control them, you can purchase units that specialize in doing one effect very well.

An effects box with a headphone jack lets you practice any time in complete silence. When inspiration strikes at two in the morning, you can turn on the reverb and play like you're in the middle of the Grand Canyon.

Everybody else can sleep.

Erin Shrader is the lutherie editor of Strings *and* Teen Strings *magazines.*

CHAPTER 13

STICK TO IT

Basic bow care is as easy as one, two, three

By Erin Shrader

"People are endlessly creative in the ways they find to break things," longtime San Francisco violin maker and dealer Roland Feller once said. While the story of every bow that comes in for repair is unique, it doesn't take too many years in the repair shop to learn the repertoire of things that commonly happen to bows: broken tip plates, stripped eyelets, wobbly frogs, heads that have snapped off, pearl that has worn away, sticks that have lost their camber or been warped from losing too much hair on one side.

Some accidents are, of course, unavoidable, but a lot of damage, including the kind of wear and tear that ruins a bow over time, can be prevented. And it's not that hard. The everyday basics of bow care could be reduced to three simple rules: be careful where you set it down, keep it clean, and loosen the hair when you're not playing. Developing good bow-care habits, plus an occasional examination for wear and tear, should keep your stick in good working order for a long time.

> Losing hairs on one side of the stick pulls unevenly on the stick, eventually warping the bow.

Keep It Safe

The bow is most vulnerable when it's out of the case and out of your hands so be conscientious about where you set it. Never leave your bow on the edge of your music stand, on the edge of the table where it could be bumped by a passerby, or if you're a cellist or bassist, sitting on the ribs of your instrument. And no tapping the music stand! This might seem, well, obvious, but . . . . Enough said.

Less obvious and potentially more dangerous is leaving the bow (and the fiddle) sitting across an open case. This might seem more desirable than setting them on a table, but one fall of the lid and your bow is dented, if you're lucky, or broken in two if you're not. That's not to mention what might happen to the fiddle.

If you do drop your bow, examine it immediately. If the ivory tip is damaged, have it replaced. A cracked or broken tip leaves the head vulnerable to further damage. Look for vertical cracks on the flat back of the head and hairline fractures hiding in the grain along the sides. Sometimes the damage is nearly invisible, breaking hours or weeks later, seemingly for no reason. Check the stick, including the button end of the stick, another vulnerable spot. Some breaks can't be repaired, others can, but some repairs may be more expensive than the bow warrants.

If you find cracks, loosen the bow hair and have it looked at by a professional repairer.

Keep It Clean

Hand washing before playing does more than just remove the dirt and oils that gunk up the hair at the end of the bow. Washing removes sweat, which corrodes metal, dissolves pearl, and eats through wood. As you can imagine, these types of damage can, in turn, lead to a host of other problems. Everyone's body chemistry is different, so this may be more of a problem for some than others. Grime also works its way between the frog and the facets of the stick so that the surfaces no longer fit perfectly together. This is a small problem that can lead to more trouble down the line.

If your skin chemistry is particularly corrosive (you may notice a green tinge on the metal parts of your bow), ask your bow-repair person if you should have a protective leather strip put on the end of the stick behind the grip. Otherwise, it is entirely possible to wear all the way through the stick, ruining the bow.

Wipe off excess rosin when you're done playing, while it's still easy. But don't try to remove built-up rosin yourself. The solvent for rosin and varnish is the same: alcohol. The varnish on a bow stick is not as crucial as the varnish on a fiddle, but why court disaster? Your bow receives a thorough cleaning with each rehair, but you'll save your rehairer a lot of time and trouble by wiping it off.

Top: This hold reduces stress on eyelet. Bottom: Screw and eyelet adjust hair tension.

Make sure the surface upon which you're about to set your bow is clean. Bow hair is not impossible to clean, but it's easier to rehair than clean. Some people wash it with soap and water, but in my experience it never comes out quite the same. Also, bow hair conducts water like a wick right into the head and frog, which can cause problems. I tried a commercially available bow-hair cleaner without much success. The package didn't list the ingredients, but again, the solvent for rosin is alcohol, and it was hard to keep the liquid off the stick.

A Few Hair-Care Tips

When tightening and loosening the hair, hold the bow with your thumb firmly across the pearl slide while turning the button. This hold reinforces the proper relationship between the frog and stick, reducing wear on the eyelet and the stick.

The bow is a stick that holds hair under tension. If you look at the bow from the side, you see a long, gradual curve with the low point roughly near the middle, with the high points being the head and frog at each end. That curve is called the camber. It will look slightly different on every bow. As you tighten the bow, the hair moves away from the stick, pulling that curve a little straighter. The camber returns to its relaxed shape as you loosen the hair. Watch as you loosen the hair and you'll learn to see when all the tension has left the stick.

Stop loosening there; the hair shouldn't be flopping around.

Always remember to loosen the hair when you're done playing. Constant tension will, eventually, pull the camber out of the stick. The bow may seem like it's lost something in tone or feel. It is possible to have a bow re-cambered by heating the stick through and bending it, but this is a delicate and potentially dangerous operation. The heated bow can break, no matter how experienced the bow maker doing the job. The feel may also change after re-cambering.

Changes in humidity play havoc with your bow hair. In fact, your shop may ask where you live or if you will be traveling to another climate when you bring it in for a rehair. They're not being nosy! Hair that is the perfect length in temperate Seattle, in the western part of Washington, can become short enough to pull the head off if taken to arid Spokane, in the eastern side of the state. Or the same rehair could be too long to tighten the bow during an Alabama summer. This can be a problem especially with string students who get a rehair from their home shop and then take it back to college or summer camp in a different climate.

DID YOU KNOW?

"There are three important things to consider in choosing a bow," renowned Parisian bow maker STÉPHANE THOMASACHOR once said, "No. 1 is sound, No. 2 is sound, and No. 3 is sound." Of course, you'll also want to consider firmness, flexibilty, and weight. Before you shop, assess the weaknesses of your current bow and determine what you want your new bow to accomplish. And remember that no single bow is likely to be ideal for everything (solo work, chamber music, and so on) or to perform well in every environment (what are the sound qualities of the performance space?). So you most likely will need several bows to meet your various needs.

When the hair seems to lose its grip, becomes too stretched out, or loses too many hairs, especially on one side, it's time for a rehair. Losing hairs on one side of the stick pulls unevenly on the stick, eventually warping the bow. Straightening requires heating the bow, just like re-cambering.

If you're breaking hairs constantly, it means that something about the player-bow-instrument combination isn't working. It may be time to consider a different bow, to start looking for an instrument that gives you the sound you're striving for, or to examine your technique.

When you take the bow in for a rehair, the repairer will probably examine the bow with you in person to detect any faults that may create a problem during rehairing and to make a note of any pre-existing damage. He or she may point out a worn thumb leather, a worn eyelet, or other maintenance issues. Have these problems taken care of promptly: they can lead to more serious (and expensive) damage. The luthiers typically do this inspection to protect themselves from liability, but it is also an opportunity for you to ask any questions and learn what the experts see when they look at a bow. It will help you maintain this bow properly and you'll learn what to look for when it's time to shop for another bow.

TIPS FROM THE TOP

You have to make "human sounds" from your stringed instrument or people will not be able to listen to you play. My teacher taught me that.

— *Nick, 14, cello*

CHAPTER 14

ADVICE FROM THE MAESTRO

Itzhak Perlman says, sometimes, less is best

By James Reel

Old joke: How do you get to Carnegie Hall? Practice, practice, practice. But according to Itzhak Perlman, that's exactly the wrong way to get to Juilliard or any other competitive school.

"Whenever a student asks me for my autograph," he claims, "I don't say, 'Best wishes.' I say, 'Practice slowly!' Practicing is really the main component in achieving something very satisfying when you play any stringed instrument, but the problem with practice is sometimes people put in the time, they've practiced four hours, five hours a day, and can't understand why it isn't getting any better.

"It comes down to listening. What are you listening for when you practice?

"Here's my favorite example of how not to practice: You have a couple of notes that are out of tune, and you repeat them over and over for 20 minutes and it's not working, and while you were doing that, the bow was going in all bad directions because you weren't paying attention to your bow because you were only paying attention to your left hand. So your left hand is not working well yet, and you've practiced for 20 minutes with the bow wrong.

"So now you have to undo that, but you're not paying attention to the intonation, so you've practiced for 20 minutes out of tune.

DID YOU KNOW?

Playing symphonic music on just three strings: it's an often-repeated tale. On Nov. 18, 1995, violinist ITZHAK PERLMAN reportedly came onstage to give a concert at Avery Fisher Hall at Lincoln Center in New York City. Just after the orchestra began playing, Perlman broke a string. "You could hear it snap," the *Houston Chronicle* reported. "It went off like gunfire across the room . . . . He waited a moment, closed his eyes and then signaled the conductor to begin again. The orchestra began, and he played from where he had left off." Amazing, huh? Just one catch: according to snopes.com, this event never happened. Perlman didn't appear at Avery Fisher that night and though he once performed stand-up comedy after breaking a string while performing on *Sesame Street*, there's no evidence he ever modulated on the fly at Avery Fisher Hall.

Itzhak Perlman

"So just reduce it to small increments, two or three bars, and try to get a hold of everything at the same time. It's difficult to concentrate on everything. You can accomplish a lot more in less time. Practicing slowly is extremely important. Then you can figure out what's going on.

"Nothing escapes you."

CHAPTER 15

SPREAD YOUR WINGS

3 tips on making the most out of your music education

By Joshua Bell

Before Joshua Bell, 39, became an internationally known violin virtuoso with an Emmy and several Grammy Awards on his mantel, not to mention a starring role in the Oscar-winning score to The Red Violin, *he was a bright-eyed teen (albeit a college kid with a rapidly growing résumé) schlepping his fiddle around the sprawling Indiana University campus and dreaming about his future. Bell took a few moments to reflect on his own experience there and to offer three suggestions to teens looking to make the most out of their string education.*

—Editor

Joshua Bell

1. Think about the Big Picture

You see students in some of these big music schools who go through their entire tenure without ever thinking about chamber music or orchestral excerpts, choosing instead to think only about playing concertos and being a soloist. It's always dangerous to offer advice because you don't want to tone down someone's enthusiasm for that, but at the same time I've heard of famous violinists going into a classroom and saying, "I'll tell you right now that none of you will ever make it as a soloist." It may be drastic to say something like that, but it is important to emphasize the need to learn as much as possible about playing in an orchestra and playing chamber music.

2. Open Yourself Up to New Teachers

I'm a big believer in learning from lots of people. The student/ teacher relationship is a touchy one—almost sacred. Teachers are so protective of their students that the student can go through ten years or more learning from just one person. I don't think that's a

WISE WORDS

Artistically I get to delve into some of the greatest music ever written. There is nothing more satisfying than performing a Beethoven quartet and exploring the many characters and emotions that we can interpret from his music. Socially we are able to connect with people from all walks of life. Not only do we connect with audiences at concert halls, but with people in nursing homes, hospitals, prisons, children of all ages, and so on.

—*Brandon Vamos, cellist of the Pacifica Quartet*

good idea. My teacher, Josef Gingold, always encouraged me to play for other people. There was a great student of his and of Heifetz's who is now a teacher at the University of California at Santa Barbara but who used to teach at IU. His name is Yuval Yaron, and Gingold wanted me to play for him. He wanted me play for several others, including Heifetz, though that never happened. But I think that's really important in order to broaden your skills.

3. Take Advantage of Master Classes

It always baffled me that there were students at Indiana University—this amazing university with public master classes with Gingold, János Starker, and Menachem Pressler, and so many others—who'd go their entire four years without ever having attended a class with one of these great teachers. I think that's just a shame. You need to be open to learning from a lot of other people and assimilating that information into your own philosophy of music. That's really crucial.

CHAPTER 16

ON DEVELOPING SELF-DISCIPLINE

Nicola Benedetti finds the strength to excel

By Laurence Vittes

Those sultry publicity photos of Nicola Benedetti are clearly intended to promise experiences that are as much dreamy musical ecstasy as dazzling technical virtuosity. That promise is confirmed by the young violinist's magnificent first two recordings for the Deutsche Grammophon label that signed her in 2005 to a multiyear contract well in excess of $1 million. However, when it comes to a discussion of preparing for a career as a high-flying world-class soloist, 20-year-old Benedetti reveals her practical Scottish roots.

Benedetti's native practicality was encouraged when, at the age of ten, she entered the Yehudi Menuhin School for gifted musicians. There, she worked with Natasha Boyarskaya, whom she has described as a teacher who "was very disciplined and expected me to be disciplined. I warmed very much to that. I enjoyed working incredibly hard and having another goal to reach each week."

Benedetti feels that's the kind of self-discipline that is crucial for anyone aiming to become a professional musician and who will be on his or her own from an early age.

Looking back, she reflects on the advantage of having taken her studying seriously as a preteen: "The more you do at an early stage," she says, "the more you will be able to accomplish later on, and more easily."

Her stardom seemingly assured, Benedetti now practices "sound production and tone more than anything else." And

Nicola Benedetti

while listening for "quirks of phrasing or style" is important, she says, "it is not as important as listening to your sound. Because when you listen to an instrumentalist, it's impossible not to hear her personality shine through, as if she were speaking or singing to you.

DID YOU KNOW?

By the time WOLFGANG AMADEUS MOZART turned 15, in 1771, he had 67 works to his credit, including 14 symphonies, 8 sonatas for violin and piano, and one string quartet.

"So, my priority, whenever I'm performing, recording, or rehearsing, is not to be loud or superficially impressive, but to produce the sound that my voice would make if I could speak or sing the notes."

Practice Smart

Here are a few tips from Benedetti on getting the most out of your practice time:

"Give yourself a fail-safe position by practicing more often for less time. You can accomplish more in two 15-minute practice sessions than you can in one 30-minute session.

"Concentrate on finding interesting things in the real basics of your own playing: tone production, shifting, vibrato, and, especially, relaxation.

"Look at your hands in the mirror to see if they look natural [on the instrument and bow], then rearrange them if necessary.

WISE WORDS

> A lot of what draws me to this music is the people in it, this community of musicians that I've been introduced into.
>
> —*Brittany Haas, fiddler*

"Don't worry about occasionally being too hard on yourself. It's not necessarily a bad thing, but it is also very important to sit back and see what you have achieved."

Although Benedetti is still in many ways a student, she believes deeply in giving back to the educational system, which has been her benefactor. Last year, she toured with the Edinburgh Youth Orchestra, and visited schools in both Scotland and England for the Sargent Cancer Care Practice-a-thon.

"Don't worry about occasionally being too hard on yourself."
—Nicola Benedetti

But it's not only musicians her own age she enjoys working with.

"I've been to many schools," she says, "and sometimes it's a more exciting experience when the class is of non-music students. I'll never forget one school where there was hardly any music education. I was warned that the 16 year olds I would be talking to and playing for might not be receptive. Instead, the silence when I played showed me how deeply the music made them feel, because their ears were 100 percent open."

CHAPTER 17

BE YOURSELF

5 Ways to Find Success

By Hilary Hahn

In 2001, Time *magazine hailed Hilary Hahn, 27, as "America's best young classical musician." She continues to mature as a player and is one of the most intelligent and thoughtful violinists around. We asked Hahn to share some sage advice.*

1. It doesn't matter if your teacher is famous or not; it doesn't matter if other people say you should study with your teacher or not. If you're not comfortable with a teacher, nothing is going to go well. Find someone who will work with you individually, in a very personal way. I've never had luck taking lessons from people who use an all-purpose "method." I don't like the cookie-cutter approach.

2. Find a teacher you feel safe with, but one who can still challenge you, because if you're not being challenged, you're not going to make much progress. Try to do whatever he or she suggests, even if you don't think it's the right thing at the time. This will teach you how to make something work that you think you can't do. Figure out what your teacher is aiming for, and if you strongly object to the suggested process, see if you can get the same result through a different technique. Often you can get the sound or phrasing they want in your own way.

Hilary Hahn

3. Be consistent with your practicing. It's not a matter of how many hours of practice you can squeeze into a day; it's a matter of how many days you can keep the same schedule. If you're busy one day and skip practicing, then the next day you try to practice four hours, you'll get too tired, and so you'll feel like taking the next day

off. You won't make any progress that way. Figure out how
many hours you can realistically
practice every day, even if it's
just a couple, and work out a

There is no top. There are always further heights to reach.
—*Jascha Heifetz, violinist*

schedule that you can follow every day without fail. And
don't forget to leave some time to experiment. Give yourself a little
more time than you think you'll need to practice the pieces you're
working on so you can hash out new ideas. That will give you the
flexibility you'll need when you start working with different accom-
panists or conductors every week.

4. Some people think you shouldn't exercise in ways that are different from the ways you use muscles when you play, but I disagree.
My dad was a journalist for a sports-medicine magazine, so he came
at physical activity from an athletic perspective.

"I don't like the cookie-cutter approach."
—Hilary Hahn

When I was little, he imposed an exercise routine on me: One
day I'd do 20 minutes on a rowing machine, and the next I'd do
sets of chin-ups. That developed the support muscles I need for
playing the violin, muscles I wouldn't have developed just by playing. And it got me into the habit of taking care of my body.

5. My first teacher, Mrs. [Klara] Berkovich, loved art and showed me books and postcards of pieces from the Hermitage and made me visit art museums. My next teacher, Mr. [Jascha] Brodsky, was always reading—books about music and other things—and that made me want to read, too. It's important to explore all the arts and literature; they're all integrated, and reading broadly and being familiar with other arts is a way of integrating your music with the world around you.

REACH FOR
THE STARS

I began playing the violin when I was 2 3/4 years old. There was something haunting and beautiful that pulled me to the instrument. I came to understand that the violin was capable of great pathos and that it was the instrument that most closely emulated the human voice. I began to play and I never looked back.

—*Jourdan, 15, violin*

CHAPTER 18

GOING THE DISTANCE

*Caitlin Tully is balancing the demands
of school, stage, and sports*

By James Reel

Now that she's mastered 25 concertos, performed with orchestras from Dallas to Toronto, designed much of her own concert clothing, and celebrated her 18th birthday, Caitlin Tully is ready to try something different: college.

All she has to do is figure out how she can keep her studies at Princeton University, beginning this fall, where she is as yet undecided on a major, from interfering with her concert career.

Besides all the concerto work, she has a recital in Paris coming up in spring 2007, and she has to make time for her lessons with Itzhak Perlman.

Caitlin
Tully

"It's kind of neat to do music as a job already and realize, yeah, I do like it," she says. "Now I want to figure out how to turn that into being a well-rounded adult, which is why I'm going to college while doing music as my career. How do I build a career and perform in the places and with the kinds of musicians I really want to, and not have school be detrimental in terms of scheduling? I don't know if I can do it.

"Talk to me in four years."

Caitlin hasn't gone to a regular school since she was 10, when her parents came up with a combination of college classes, private tutoring, and self-guided textbook work to get her educated while still leaving time for music. "I was lucky that I was always doing other things with other kids, but it did make it a lot easier to travel for concerts," she says.

Caitlin pronounces her Celtic first name "cat-lin," but she's not an Irish lass. She was born in Connecticut, but was brought up in Canada until her dad became head of the history department at the University of Texas. Her first awards, concerts, and appearances on radio and TV were in Canada, but now the Lone Star State claims Caitlin as one of its own: The Texas Cultural Trust Council gave her the 2005 Texas Medal of Arts Award.

> What makes the difference between Heifetz and violinists who are just pretty good is that last five percent of hard work, all the time.
>
> —Caitlin Tully

Many young people, to get as far as Caitlin has at her age, spend their childhood shut up in a room practicing all day. Caitlin acknowledges that a lot of work stands behind every concert she gives. "It's like being an athlete," she says. "A swimmer has to be in the pool for hours every day. It's true of anything you do intensely. But if I look back over the past eight years, I feel very fortunate because I've gotten to do a lot of other things and still do my music with the intensity that I want."

She's a serious runner, for one thing. "I've always been fairly athletic, and running is a great thing to do if you travel; you just stick your shoes in your bag, and you're ready," she says. "It's good for me to do something like that, where there's a lot of adrenalin. It makes me feel stronger, which makes me more into music with my body. Playing an instrument is a physical thing; running makes me more aware of my body, how my muscles are working when I play, and it's a good way to get rid of stress."

She says she doesn't get much flack from people warning her that she could hurt herself by being athletic. "I'm not inclined to

DID YOU KNOW?

Before he started writing catchy pop hooks, Canadian singer and songwriter DANIEL POWTER—best known for his sunshine mega-hit "Bad Day"—honed his musical skills playing the violin. Powter started playing at age four, accompanying his pianist mother in their home studio. In 2006, "Bad Day" became the theme song for 'American Idol' contestants booted off the show each week. Sales soared, but it turns out that Powter knows what it feels like to be bounced off of a talent show: he used to compete unsuccessfully in violin contests. He even got beat up once while walking down the street with his violin case, but he hung in there. Using those musical skills to his advantage and rising to the top of the pop charts is his sweet revenge.

go out and rollerblade, because there's a large percentage of accidents from that activity that affect the wrists. I'm conscientious about my upper body, but beyond that you just hope for good fortune. I can trip just walking, because I'm a klutz."

It all comes down to making careful choices. "I've been very lucky in that I don't think there's anything I love doing that I don't get to do because I'm a violinist," she says. "You figure out how to work music and other things into the life you have.

"For a while I liked to practice a lot in the morning, and I still do; I don't practice well in the afternoon. But now that I've been performing more in the last two or three years and have to travel, I can't have a strict schedule. I have to be flexible, and figure out how to do what needs to be done depending on what else is going on."

Caitlin is not a person who slacks off, according to her Texas coach, Jan Sloman, principal associate concertmaster of the Dallas Symphony. "Caitlin is a wonderful student," he says. "She is curious, inquisitive, and positive. She likes to see the whole picture; she wants to see how systems function. It's not just analytical, it's that she wants to get a sense of the whole process. There's no artifice about her. She is very straight-ahead and genuine. What you see is what you get.

"She has everything it takes, artistically, personally, intellectually, and emotionally, to develop as a musician and an artist. All the elements are in place for her to be a complete artist."

Caitlin knows that she's still in the process of becoming that complete artist, and that even though she's been playing the violin since age four, the hard work is by no means over. "I start to think, 'Boy, do I really have to work on intonation my entire life?' And I do," she says. "What makes the difference between Heifetz and violinists who are just pretty good is that last five percent of hard work, all the time.

"I wouldn't say I ever had burnout because of that. Sometimes after a whole lot of performances or in the summer I'll take a week or two off. I'm still playing, because it feels gross if I don't, but I'll putter around the house or go to movies and not immerse myself in music so much. It feels great for a week and then I begin to miss it.

"I have lots of interests, but I can't imagine doing anything else with my life."

CHAPTER 19

IN THE SWING OF THINGS

*Classical violinists don't play western swing. Dang!
Someone must have forgotten to tell Damian Green*

By James Reel

Want to find out Damian Green's musical hero? The 16-year-old fiddler likes to tell a joke about Jascha Heifetz, the most famous classical violinist of the 20th century. "There's this story that Heifetz was trying to get his dog into his hotel room," he says. "The manager stopped him, and the violinist puffed up and said, 'But I'm Jascha Heifetz.' The manager said, 'I don't care if you're Bob Wills, you're not bringing that dog in here.'"

Sure, Green knows his way around the classical violin; he has a lot of concertos in his fingers, and he plays in an orchestra in his native Texas. But at heart, he's less of a Jascha Heifetz fan than a keeper of the flame of the great Texas swing fiddler Bob Wills.

Wills and his Texas Playboys played country dance tunes as if they were jazz numbers. Wills didn't invent Texas swing in the 1930s, but he pretty much perfected it, and he's Damian Green's hero.

In fact, Green keeps getting compared to Wills, both in his playing and his stage presence. That's how Green wants it.

"Yes sir," he says with his polite Texas accent. "I like his overall charisma, the way he moved on stage, the way he got the audience going. I collect a bunch of Bob Wills recordings, and I listen to those a lot, and learn a lot, and I even get to play with the Texas Playboys and learn from them in person."

Damian Green

That's right. He hasn't even graduated from high school, but Green already has played with the old Bob Wills band, not to mention his touring with the famed Texas swing group Asleep at the Wheel in a tribute show called *A Ride with Bob*. The subject, you might guess, is Bob Wills. When Green, the band, and the show's other participants played at the Kennedy Center in

Washington, D.C., in September of 2006, Green even got to shake hands with a big fan of Texas swing: President George W. Bush.

None of this exactly happened overnight—Green got what you might call an early start. "I wanted to play the bass when I was two and a half year old," he says. He'd seen what that instrument and others could do because his aunt was a high-school orchestra teacher. "But I was too little for the bass, so they gave me an 1/8-size fiddle and I started with a Suzuki program."

When he was seven, Green attended a western-swing camp, where he got his first real introduction to the style. "It combines the blues, the jazz, the country, and the big-band swing all into one," Green says.

He couldn't resist.

"I love the classical stuff for the technical training," he says, "but I really enjoy playing the western swing and country jazz, to be on stage and to hear the audience—it's a different reaction."

Says Green's teacher, Bill Dick, "The thing about Damian that's most impressive to me is that he has a sense of the moment. By that I mean when he's onstage he's got the costume, he's got the moves, he's got the showbiz part of it down, but it doesn't seem cheesy. He's doing a great show and having fun doing it. But then, at his lessons, he's matter-of-fact, and he's not resistant to criticism or change. Whatever he's doing, he's doing it 100 percent and honestly. As a student he's receptive and not insecure, and onstage he's struttin' with the best of them."

He can switch styles easily, too, says Dick. "This semester he played the 16th Paganini Caprice for All State, and he's good about adjusting his bow stroke so he's not swinging Paganini. He can address whatever music's in front of him, like there's a little needle that goes wherever it needs to go whatever the repertoire is. And he's such a friendly, happy kid. His parents certainly raised a very secure kid without his being an arrogant jerk."

If anybody has reason to be arrogant, it's Damian Green. Success came to him early. When he was still a chubby-faced preteen he was called Fiddle Boy, which was also the title of his first CD. The CD cover depicted him dressed like Superman, flying through the air with a fiddle under his arm. Like fellow Texan and teen concert violinist Caitlin Tully, Green was a Texas Cultural Trust Council Young Master, an honor he received in 2006. The year before, he won the American String Teachers Association alternative-styles award in his age category. Now he's got his own band,

"The thing about Damian that's most impressive to me is that he has a sense of the moment."
—Bill Dick

and he goes around romping with Asleep at the Wheel and the Texas Playboys. Why wouldn't he be a little full of himself?

But, like his teacher says, he's not. And he knows the next few years are going to be tricky for him. Before long, he'll be too old to get by as your friendly neighborhood child prodigy. He'll have to establish a place for himself amid all the other great adult Texas-swing fiddlers out there.

He's homeschooled now, which gives him time to play gigs without missing out on his education. In a couple of years he'd like to be studying at the Berklee College of Music in Boston, which takes alternative styles as seriously as most conservatories regard classical.

And then?

According to Bill Dick, it'll be a combination of being "discovered" by the right people, and proving that he can do more than emulate his hero, Bob Wills. "The sound he's producing is going to have to be innovative," he says. "Right now he's a great mimic, but I don't think he does his own material yet. In Texas swing, I don't think he can just cover songs the way classical violinists cover the Mendelssohn concerto. If someone comes up just playing Charlie Daniels tunes, that won't make it.

"He's got the show side, and if he can spin that off into something original, that's what it would take to get him to the top of his field. He's very hardworking and very gifted; he's got things to learn, but once he picks up enough music theory to write his own stuff, the career is basically in his pocket."

That's why Green wants to go to Berklee, to develop that musical foundation. And he wants to keep learning secrets from all

> **WISE WORDS**
>
> The older I get the more fun I have. I'm amazed to think of how much fun I'll be having a few years from now. It really does just keep on getting better. —*Jeremy Kittel, fiddler*

kinds of violinists, classical and jazz, living and dead—Itzhak Perlman, Stéphane Grappelli, Joe Venuti, and Stuff Smith all are in his iPod. "I try to keep myself well-rounded," Green says.

And, he points out, even though he's gotten famous around Texas pretty fast, he's had to work at it. "I never take time off from practicing," he says. "If I'm getting ready for something special, like a concert or a competition, I spend four or five hours a day working on it. If I'm just maintaining, I spend two-and-a-half to three hours a day. Bill Dick gives me a bunch of exercises for speed and accuracy, a lot of arpeggios and basic scales, and then sometimes different études like the Rode and the Paganini caprices; those help me maintain my technique.

"Before a concert or a competition, we get the guys in the band together and have a rehearsal. We play a couple of hours and run over all our tunes and make sure we know everything and don't get nervous. Usually in a show I feel a lot more loose than in a competition, because in a show I feel like I have more control over what I'm doing. In competitions I have to follow a more structured pattern."

So he's got all the right habits and strategies. Bill Dick repeats that there's just that one more thing he has to develop.

"He needs theory," he says. "That's what's going to unlock his creative side, and open him up to his own voice and his own music and his own career."

CHAPTER 20
VIENNESE WALTZ

English violinist Chloë Hanslip may be walking in Mozart's footsteps, but she's definitely not trying to fill his shoes

By Inge Kjemtrup

Who would ever want to be a violin prodigy? Sure, audiences won't be able to get enough of you when you're a sweet little thing powering your way through Paganini on your pint-size violin, but as soon as you advance past the cute stage, the next prodigy is right behind you, ready to take your place. There's a long list of wunderkinds who've hung up their Strads when they hit their teens.

English violinist Chloë Hanslip is one of the exceptions. Confident and poised, the 19-year-old former prodigy is enjoying a burgeoning international solo concert career and, with several recordings already under her belt, has recently released a well-received disc on the Naxos label featuring the John Adams Violin

Concerto, making her internationally known.

The critics can't seem to get enough of her. Reviewing her performance of the Sibelius Violin Concerto with the Bavarian Radio Symphony Orchestra under Mariss Jansons, the *British Independent* newspaper wrote, "Hanslip produces a full-blooded sound: her wide-spaced vibrato and powerful resonances rendered her an expressive, idiosyncratic advocate of the Sibelius: intense, passionate, not without cheeky waywardness. Her

dazzling technical proficiency made sparks fly in the finale."

Born in Surrey, to the south of London, Hanslip's life as a prodigy began when, just able to walk, she toddled up to the piano and tapped out tunes. Her older sister, then a piano student at the Royal Academy of Music in London, was not pleased. "She would get very indignant and say, 'She's ruining my music!'" says Hanslip. "My parents didn't want another pianist in the house, so they started me on the violin."

Hanslip began studying the violin alongside her mother, as is the tradition in the Suzuki method. However, her mother soon bowed out. "After six weeks she was told she could give up because I was better than her," laughs Hanslip. At five, she played for the legendary British violinist Yehudi Menuhin, who sent her to Natasha Boyarskaya, the main violin teacher at the Menuhin School.

"I didn't like lessons very much," remembers Hanslip, "but I'm incredibly grateful to her now, because she's the person who really gave me the basis of my technique."

studying with Gerhard Schulz has brought her closer to understanding the great German masters.

At seven, Hanslip played for Zakhar Bron, the great Russian teacher whose pupils include violinists Maxim Vengerov and Vadim Repin. Bron and Hanslip immediately hit it off. "The fact that I was living in Surrey and he was living in northern Germany didn't really bother either of us," she says. "But my father said, 'Professor Bron, we have to talk about this [traveling],' and Bron said, 'What is there to talk about?'

"So my mother and I moved to Germany when I was nearly eight."

By Hanslip's account, her lessons with Bron were bliss, but going to the German school was painful. Hanslip was academically ahead, but a step behind socially because she didn't know German (she now speaks it fluently). She recalls, "The other children had trouble accepting a little eight-year-old prodigy with big glasses who played the violin and who was English," and so the young Hanslip was bullied.

Returning to an English prep school two years later wasn't the solution, as she was still academically ahead of her contemporaries. Plus, says Hanslip, "I was never there! So I was home educated from the age of ten." She thrived as a homeschooled student, getting high marks on the standardized tests and, later on, was offered a place at Oxford University.

She turned it down in favor of the violin.

She's had a few other detours from the prodigy path, however, such as playing a prodigy in a film when she was ten, in *Onegin*, which co-starred Ralph Fiennes and Liv Tyler. Hanslip loved every minute of it—except for not getting to wear any makeup. "When I got there, they said, 'You have a perfect Russian complexion, you don't need any makeup.'

"I was so disappointed!"

She didn't get any lines, but Hanslip had her own artistic challenge: "They gave me ten days to learn the 'Devil's Trill' sonata [by Tartini]!"

This past September, Hanslip received the Shakespeare Scholarship from the German Alfred Toepfer Foundation, for which she was nominated by Welsh baritone Bryn Terfel, a good friend. She'll use the money to fund her lessons in Vienna with violinist Gerhard Schulz of the Alban Berg Quartet. Studying with Schulz has brought her closer to understanding the great German masters. Plus, she loves "the whole feeling of culture and the atmosphere" in Vienna, which in her case includes walking by Mozart's house every day.

The diminutive Hanslip is also a car fanatic, a passion she traces back to hours of looking out train and bus windows in Germany and counting the number of Mercedes-Benzes on the autobahn.

When she's not performing, studying, or practicing ("I try to get in five to six hours a day"), Hanslip can be found exercising at her local gym (she particularly likes Bhangra/Bollywood-style dancing), instant messaging, reading, or listening to a mix of music on her iPod. Her eclectic play list includes UK house-music band the Basement Jaxx, an Oregon-based band named Pink Martini (which blends classical chamber, Cuban, and French film music), the Black Eyed Peas, Rat Pack alum Sammy Davis, Jr., classical violinists Nathan Milstein and Ida Haendel, and Pierre Fournier playing the Dvořák Cello Concerto.

The diminutive Hanslip is also a car fanatic, a passion she traces back to hours of looking out train and bus windows in Germany and counting the number of Mercedes-Benzes on the autobahn. The night before we spoke, she'd been at the launch of the new BMW 3 series ("beautiful, beautiful car") and earlier in the year she'd attended a Formula One race with her father.

She is on her second Mini Cooper. Her first Mini was a write-off after a 40-ton truck slammed into it on the M25 motorway. "I got smashed in the face by the airbag cover, but other than that I was fine. Quite why I'm here, I'm not sure," she remarks, adding dryly, "Minis are extremely well-built cars."

If good fortune played a role in Hanslip's surviving that car accident, she's happy to spread the good fortune, regularly playing concerts for charity.

"I think it's so important for me to give back. I especially love doing things with children," she says, recalling her experience of playing at London's Great Ormond Street Children's Hospital.

"There was the most beautiful little girl called Elana, who was eight or nine and I played for her. She had a rare form of cancer."

Two weeks after Hanslip played for her, Elana passed away. "To know that I made her happy is so special," she says.

It seems that making people happy will remain an important part of Hanslip's life as she develops both as a person and a musician, going far beyond the narrow stereotype of "former child prodigy."

CHAPTER 21

IN THE MOMENT

*For Nigel Armstrong, the emotional connection
to the music is paramount*

By David Templeton

Nigel Armstrong is in a trance. That's what it looks like, anyway, when Armstrong—violin in place, eyes half-closed in concentration—launches the fiery last Allegro in Saint-Saëns' Rondo Capriccioso, his sautillé bouncing with remarkable cleanness as his face reacts to the twists and turns of the music.

It's a lot like watching a video of someone on a roller coaster; you've probably noticed that nine out of ten riders will be screaming and laughing and waving their arms, while one person just sits there, not shrieking, not laughing, but clearly reacting, trance-like, to every ascent and descent, soaking up every sensation along the way. In the end, it is usually the person with that look who experi-

135

Nigel Armstrong

ences the ride most fully, and Nigel Armstrong has that look on his face right now.

Today, the 16-year-old violinist is the special guest soloist for an afternoon performance with the American Philharmonic-Sonoma County, performing at Spreckels Performing Arts Center in Rohnert Park, California, about 40 miles north of San Francisco. His performance also includes Saint-Saëns' Havanaise. Later, Nigel admits he lets himself get very involved in the music he is playing, and appreciates players who do not sacrifice emotional connection for mere technical proficiency.

"It was very fun to play those pieces with that orchestra," he says a few days later. "And it was especially fun to work with the American Philharmonic's conductor, Gabriel Sakakeeny, because he has so much passion and enthusiasm for the music.

"I like that."

Armstrong is one of those players who's been called a prodigy since before he learned to ride a bike. He began playing violin at the age of five, but requested lessons at four after hearing violin music coming from the house across the street, where the neighborhood violin teacher lived. He started high-school math and science classes at 12, and when featured on the popular National Public Radio program *From the Top*—playing Dvořák's Romance in

> "I think it's important for a musician to develop different interests, to create a life aside from music." —Nigel Armstrong

F minor, Op. 11—reporter Hayley Goldbach challenged Armstrong's statement that his favorite thing to read was British newsmagazine the *Economist*. His response to Goldbach's impromptu news quiz proved that he really did read the topical magazine.

He debuted professionally with the Berkeley Symphony two years later, performing as the symphony's inaugural Young Artist Award recipient. Since then, he has won a closetful of awards, including some for his own compositions; in 2002, he earned Honorable Mention in the ASCAP Young Composers Morton Gould Awards for a composition entitled Song of the Zoonks.

Originally from the rural town of Sonoma (not far from Rohnert Park), Armstrong is a junior at Walnut Hill School in Massachusetts, a private boarding-school for the arts that focuses on music, theater, ballet, modern dance, creative writing, and the visual arts. Renowned as one of the best "finishing schools" for artistically oriented kids, the school, located about 25 minutes south of Boston, attracts students from all over the world.

Armstrong is a long way from home, but he says that living in the Boston area, surrounded by like-minded students—more than 25 of them are also violinists—is a good experience, though much different from Northern California.

"The richness of the culture at Walnut Hill is really powerful," he says. "It's interesting that the international students, a lot of them, end up adopting the attitudes of the culture here, which is a mix of East Coast attitude and a kind of high-school-artist attitude.

"It's a very high-charged energy around here."

Of course, the Boston area affords many cultural opportunities. "Musically, there is a lot more going on here, in general," he says. "A lot of interesting things are happening in Boston."

He visits the city at least twice a week for chamber-music coaching, and is frequently able to attend concerts in his spare time, of which he doesn't have much.

And that's how he likes it.

With so many performances at school and a number of auditions lined up, his primary priority is to develop a strong repertoire of audition pieces, all while continuing to hone his musical chops, and work on his own compositions.

"The coolest thing I'm doing right now is my own music," he says. "I really enjoy creating."

Occasionally, Armstrong even manages to have a little non-musical fun, though there are those who might challenge his definition of the word "fun." When not practicing the violin, he enjoys studying world-philosophy and the occasional European novel (he's recently been reading the works of the French philosopher Voltaire and just finished novelist Umberto Eco's *The Name of the Rose*). He is fond of playing logic games such as chess, Go, and the Chinese variants of Go.

> ## DID YOU KNOW?
> Famed physicist ALBERT EINSTEIN was known to carry his violin nearly everywhere he went. The scientist's mother insisted he take violin lessons at a young age, which Einstein initially found tedious. But the young man stuck with it and grew to love and cherish his violin. Photos of Einstein playing violin are nearly as famous as his $E=Mc^2$ formula.

As for sports, all things considered, soccer is his favorite game.

"I'm not very good at soccer," he allows, with a laugh, "but I like playing soccer anyway. I like that it's a team sport, and involves thinking as a unit rather than as a single person. I think it's important for a musician to develop different interests, to create a life aside from music. Influenced by music, yes, but not focused only on music."

Laughing, he adds, "I don't really know how to do that, but I do think it's a good idea."

Armstrong is not certain what his steps will be beyond high school. He intends to be a professional musician—and is already well on his way—but is still unsure whether he sees himself as a soloist, a member of an orchestra, or part of a chamber ensemble—all of which he has enjoyed.

"I'm keeping my options open. I could be happy doing many things," he says.

> 6 Music is not just an intellectual exercise. It is an emotional exercise, too. 9
>
> –Nigel Armstrong

As for college, he's applying to Harvard, but is keeping his options open there as well. "I don't know what school I really want to go to," he says. "Actually, 'I don't know' is something I've been saying and thinking a lot lately. I've got a lot of things to figure out."

It's not too surprising—especially coming from someone who's fluent in the philosophical musings of controversial French rationalists—that Armstrong has strong opinions on many subjects, none stronger than his ideas about music. Mainly, he is committed to classical music. Secondly, for a teen who is interested in so many intellectual pursuits, his approach to music is surprisingly poetic and emotional.

"One thing I find very important in my own playing," he explains, "is to keep remembering that music is not just an intellectual exercise. It is an emotional exercise, too. I find that lacking in many musicians, professional or not, and especially in young players, where classical training is often just a step to something else, away from classical music and toward something else: maybe rock 'n' roll or traditional music. I really do believe that the love of classical music is being lost, even among young classically trained players.

"Rock 'n' roll doesn't appeal to me on an emotional level as much as classical music does," he continues. "It doesn't resonate at a higher level for me. Rock and classical are different art forms and they both have their unique appeals, but I prefer the intensity of classical music. I find that classical music is thoughtful and contemplative—but it's very direct, and that's where the intensity comes in. It's not relaxed music. I'm intense when I play, because the emotions are intense, and for me, that should be the goal of a musician: to experience fully the emotions you are playing."

Asked to boil that down to a short, simple piece of advice for other young players, Armstrong is silent for several seconds. Finally, he says, "A lot of young players make the mistake of focusing only on cultivating their expertise instead of focusing on what makes the music so wonderful. My advice is to remember why you are a musician.

"The music is the moment," he says. "Enjoy yourself."

ACE OF BASS

Elizabeth Dorman approaches the future
one step at a time

By Tiffany Martini

The double bass 18-year-old Elizabeth Dorman plays dwarfs her five-foot-three frame by more than a foot, a fact that draws frequent comments that are the source of some irritation—even if Dorman does on occasion make that observation herself. "Everybody says that!" she exclaims while standing in the lobby of Davies Symphony Hall, home to the San Francisco Symphony and a place where Dorman splits her time between playing double bass and piano in the organization's youth orchestra. "I think the bass is taller than most people," she adds.

She makes a good point.

In fact, Dorman makes lots of good points.

Elizabeth Dorman

Level-headed, insightful, and infinitely cheerful, the teen string player appears to have an extraordinarily bright future ahead of her, but Dorman isn't really thinking about that for the moment. "I'm not sure what I want to do. I love the instrument," she says. "Right now I'm just going to try to study as much as I can and leave those kinds of decisions for grad school."

Perhaps it's easy to be so even-keeled when success has seemed a constant friend. Four years ago, Dorman scored a sweet deal when she tried out for the prestigious SFS Youth Orchestra. Not only did the teenager pass the audition, she won the coveted principal bassist seat.

In recent years, she's also nabbed honors at the Ross McKee Competition, Young Artists Beethoven Competition, and, most recently, the 2005 San Francisco Youth Orchestra Competition.

Music critic Joshua Kosman of the *San Francisco Chronicle* praised Dorman for her delivery of Bartók's Third Concerto, noting that the performance was "as striking for its restraint as its technical assurance." He also called her "unnervingly precocious."

He got that right.

Yet her career as a double bassist almost didn't happen. At age 12, Dorman—who'd been playing violin for eight years—developed a wanderlust for the cello. That dream proved short-lived. Her middle-school orchestra teacher informed the ingénue there were just too many cellos already in the school's ensemble.

"So he stuck me out in the hallway with a scale book [and a bass]," Dorman says, "and I've been playing ever since."

> "It doesn't seem like music and competitions go together, but unfortunately they are necessary."
> —Elizabeth Dorman

A graduate of San Francisco's prestigious School of the Arts, one of two public schools that are exclusively competitive entry, and a student at the San Francisco Conservatory of Music since age 5, Dorman initially found school to be a bit tedious. "I always wanted to be taken out of school so I could just practice," she says. "But my mom thought it was really important, so I could get socialized. [The School of the Arts] was a good compromise."

She didn't understand the reasoning then, but she now understands that staying among her peers in school has helped her become a well-rounded, independent person. Her involvement in orchestras—including her high-school orchestra, the San Francisco Youth Symphony, and an orchestra at the San Francisco Conservatory—has given her a system of support, even when she gets to step into the forefront.

"I love playing concertos," she says. "It's impossible to get nervous when there's so many people on stage with you. It's like a great social event, playing with the orchestra."

That love of teamwork may explain why Dorman isn't too keen on the competition circuit. "It's so subjective," she says of competitions. "How can you say that one person is better than everyone else? It doesn't seem like music and competitions go together, but unfortunately they are necessary.

"So it's important to do them, but it doesn't mean you have to like them."

This fall, Dorman began her sophomore year at the San Francisco Conservatory of Music, where she majors in both bass and piano performance. The newly relocated conservatory is the only college to which she applied.

> ## WISE WORDS
>
> When you're playing fiddle music, you're always improvising grace notes and bowing, improvising around the notes, like Baroque players used to do. I think my classical playing is more spontaneous and intuitive than it may have been had I not had that background.
>
> —*Carol Cook, violist*

Dorman is still undecided as to whether she will ultimately choose one instrument over the other, or what her future will bring. But jumping into the unknown doesn't perplex Dorman; she strolls the unpaved roads that lay before her with the calm of a true professional.

"I think there's time [to decide the role bass will play in her life]," she says. "I think a lot of young people don't realize that. Because you're not just playing music when you are in high school or when you are a kid—you could do this your whole life."

RESOURCES

Whether you're looking for advice, sheet music, or a place to connect with other string players, you'll find tons of websites that cater to your every string-playing whim. Check out these online resources next time you're on the Web.*

Teen Strings and *Strings* Online

Your one-stop shop for all things strings! Find practice and performance tips, profiles, gear info, games, polls, and forums to chat with other string players. And when it's time to find that perfect summer-study program or next step in your strings education, don't forget to search our summer-study guide and education databases. *www.teenstrings.com; www.stringsmagazine.com*

Free online resources

ASTA—American String Teacher Association sponsors the National Orchestra Festival, solo and alternative-styles competitions, and instrument outreach programs for kids. *www.astaweb.com*

American Viola Society—Yeah, there's a great big community of viola players out there. This site offers links to viola societies around the globe. *www.americanviolasociety.org*

Remember, if you're under 18, be sure to check with the parents before you surf these sites.

Bowed Radio—A program that uses a podcast format and releases a new episode each week. Programs run the gamut from string quartets to jazz violinists, heavy-metal string trios to hip-hop fiddlers. Hear the latest in the world of string playing. *www.bowed. org; www.myspace.com/bowedradio*

International Society of Bassists—The bottom line on all things bass. *www.isbworldoffice.com*

Internet Cello Society—Boy those cellists can be chatty! One of the most extensive—and active—online forums around, offering a wealth of information. *www.cello.org*

New York Philharmonic Kids Zone!—Meet the conductor and members of the NY Phil, play games, compose music, and learn about the orchestra's instruments. Ringtones of audio clips recorded at live concerts are also available for purchase. Also, if you're between the ages of 12 and 17, you'll find discounted tickets for special NY Phil performances. *www.nyphilkids.org; www.nyphil. org/ringtones; www.nyphil.org*

The Primrose International Viola Archive at Brigham Young University—Find information on violist William Primrose himself, as well as extensive viola resources. *http://music.lib.byu.edu/PIVA/*

Rachel Barton Pine—Get info on this violin soloist's instrument-loan and scholarship programs, along with links to her weekly blog, podcast, and YouTube video channel. You can visit her MySpace page as well at *www.myspace.com/rachelbartonpine. www. rachelbartonpine.com*

San Francisco Symphony Kids' Site—Find out what's up at the symphony, learn about the instruments, and check out the music lab—you can even compose your own song. *www.sfskids.org*

Violin Masterclass—The Sassmannshaus Tradition for Violin Playing. Tap into an extensive collection of lessons, performance files, info on competitions and auditions, and lots more. *www.violinmasterclass.com*

The Violin Site—Looking for free downloadable violin sheet music? Want to brush up on the history of the violin or learn a new way to memorize music? This site offers links to a host of online resources. *www.theviolinsite.com*

Violinist.com—A weekly low-down on the hottest news, developments, and trends in the string world; savvy bloggers with a wide spectrum of experience; and discussion forums where you can weigh in. *www.violinist.com*

Sheet Music

Greenblatt & Seay—Got bitten by the trad bug? Here's a source of sheet music for fiddle, viola, and cello. *www.mastercall.com/g-s/*

Freehand Music—Find thousands of downloadable pieces of affordable string music. *www.freehandmusic.com*

Mona Lisa Sound—Find some rockin' string quartet music. *www.monalisasound.com*

Sheetmusic Plus—Another comprehensive resource for sheet music online. *www.sheetmusicplus.com*

Straight from the Publishers—These publishers are the source of tons of music, so check them out. Alfred Publishing, *www.alfred. com;* Hal Leonard Publishing, *www.halleonard.com;* Mel Bay Publishing, *www.melbay.com*

Getting Out There

Music Teachers National Association—The MTNA hosts National Student Competitions throughout the country. *www.mtna.org*

Young Musicians Program—Chamber Music Society of Lincoln Center provides teen chamber ensembles an opportunity to work with renowned musicians and master teachers, in preparation for a professional performance experience. Contact Andrew Berger at *aberger@chambermusicsociety.org.*

Saving the World

Children Helping Children—15-year-old Jourdan Urbach has raised over $1 million to help kids with medical problems throughout the United States. Find out how you can help. *www.children-helpingchildren.net*

International Pernambuco Conservation Intitiative-USA—Find out what you can do to help save this endangered bow wood. *www.ipci-usa.org*